Out of Body Experience

The Ultimate Guide to Traveling Outside Your Body, Astral Projection, and Journeying Beyond the Matrix

© Copyright 2025 - All rights reserved.

The content contained within this book may not be reproduced, duplicated, or transmitted without direct written permission from the author or the publisher.

Under no circumstances will any blame or legal responsibility be held against the publisher or author for any damages, reparation, or monetary loss due to the information contained within this book, either directly or indirectly.

Legal Notice:

This book is copyright-protected. It is only for personal use. You cannot amend, distribute, sell, use, quote, or paraphrase any part of the content within this book without the consent of the author or publisher.

Disclaimer Notice:

Please note the information contained within this document is for educational and entertainment purposes only. All effort has been executed to present accurate, up-to-date, reliable, and complete information. No warranties of any kind are declared or implied. Readers acknowledge that the author is not engaging in the rendering of legal, financial, medical, or professional advice. The content within this book has been derived from various sources. Please consult a licensed professional before attempting any techniques outlined in this book.

By reading this document, the reader agrees that under no circumstances is the author responsible for any losses, direct or indirect, that are incurred as a result of the use of the information contained within this document, including, but not limited to, errors, omissions, or inaccuracies.

Your Free Gift
(only available for a limited time)

Thanks for getting this book! If you want to learn more about various spirituality topics, then join Mari Silva's community and get a free guided meditation MP3 for awakening your third eye. This guided meditation mp3 is designed to open and strengthen ones third eye so you can experience a higher state of consciousness. Simply visit the link below the image to get started.

https://spiritualityspot.com/meditation

Or, Scan the QR code!

Table of Contents

INTRODUCTION 1
CHAPTER 1: THE MATRIX AND HOW ASTRAL PROJECTION CAN HELP YOU ESCAPE 5
CHAPTER 2: THE QUANTUM SCIENCE OF OUT-OF-BODY EXPERIENCES 15
CHAPTER 3: PREPARING FOR A JOURNEY BEYOND THE BODY 27
CHAPTER 4: YOUR FIRST OBE ON THE ASTRAL PLANE 38
CHAPTER 5: EXPLORING DIMENSIONS BEYOND THE EARTHLY MATRIX 50
CHAPTER 6: OVERCOMING FEAR AND BARRIERS TO ASTRAL TRAVEL 63
CHAPTER 7: WORKING WITH ENERGY AND STAYING PROTECTED 75
CHAPTER 8: INTEGRATING YOUR OBES 87
CONCLUSION 99
HERE'S ANOTHER BOOK BY MARI SILVA THAT YOU MIGHT LIKE 104
YOUR FREE GIFT (ONLY AVAILABLE FOR A LIMITED TIME) 105
REFERENCES 106
IMAGE SOURCES 112

Introduction

Do you often catch yourself wanting to understand the meaning of life? Does it feel like you're going through the motions with each chapter of your life, feeling like some are too brief? Maybe some pages even seem to have been ripped out of the Book of Life. It's like there's some hidden conspiracy, some big secret that was once planted in the soil of what you are and then never allowed to grow branches and flourish.

Have you ever wondered what it all means and wanted to find a way to make sense of your concerns and this curious world? Perhaps you've sought answers from many different people and places, only to come away even more confused. They might come up with a multitude of factors for why you feel this way, and yet none of them seem to give you the clarity you long for. One might describe this as feeling trapped in the Matrix and, like Neo, you just know there's more to life.

Your personal experiences in this physical world might have left you confused and lost, and painful lessons never seem to provide much solace. Maybe you have this inkling that there's more to the world than what you're being told. Like in the movie The Matrix, there's a realm beyond what we see and touch daily. These unanswered questions stifle you. This is completely normal. It is the start of your awakening. No longer can anyone pull the wool over your eyes.

Our ideas of the world aren't normally shaped by our perception of truth. They're inherited from upbringing, parents, siblings, culture, religion, or society. People then assume these beliefs are a given and untouchable, even if they don't make sense to you, but this only hinders the efforts of self-discovery.

This is not just an introduction but an invitation to those seeking knowledge, clarity, and an opportunity for realization. There is a solution to all your unresolved problems, and that is an out-of-body experience.

So, what exactly is an out-of-body experience (OBE)?

It is the ability to separate from your physical body, tap into your unconscious, and ascend with your astral body as you travel to other dimensions. It is a chance for you to see the world unfolding beyond the Matrix, understand the poetry of the universe, and grow into the person you know you're meant to be. It is proof that growth does not have to be sharp and painful. It can be a quiet lesson, a soft comfort.

This book is the ultimate guide to traveling outside your body and journeying beyond. It is perfect for the curious, open-minded, and eager reader. Your mind will be opened to the spirituality, metaphysics, and purpose of out-of-body travel.

Those who want to find their true potential and achieve their goals will benefit from the knowledge in this book. An OBE can help you discover your needs and how to meet them. It will also help you identify the root cause of your doubts and whatever else is holding you back so you can let go of behaviors and beliefs that don't serve you.

This book is not just a pile of information; it provides actionable techniques for you to make sense of the world. You can embrace the mystery of life and expand your awareness beyond physical reality. *You do this through astral projection.*

Astral projection combines science, philosophy, and spirituality. It is the true way to escape the Matrix. It is the path to explore spiritual realms beyond your physical world. It can help you find your sense of self and provide answers to all kinds of questions you have about life.

Through astral projection, your unconscious self is revealed and connects with parts of the universe you never knew existed. Your unconscious can travel the world and even into outer space. You will feel like you've never felt before and discover what was once thought undiscoverable. You will broaden your perspective through a spiritual experience that can connect you to deceased loved ones and introduce you to other spiritual beings.

You will understand the world around you and your place in it. You will see there is more to you than your physical body. You will challenge your predetermined beliefs and improve your understanding of life, earth, space, and time.

This book will ensure you find your purpose and achieve it. It will help you have a successful OBE and overcome your fears and anything blocking you from living life to the fullest.

The philosophical aspects of astral travel will also be introduced. This guide will help you reconnect with your loved ones, better understand the afterlife, and walk you through the scientific process of astral projection, appealing to spiritual seekers and winning over even the biggest skeptics.

An OBE isn't just about having faith but practical knowledge. Therefore, this book offers insight into the study of energy and the science, history, and fundamental principles of astral projection. With hands-on OBE exercises ideal for the complete beginner and the more advanced astral travelers, you will confidently prepare for a journey beyond the body.

You will be given tools to escape the Matrix through astral projection and explore dimensions beyond. You will know everything there is to know about your first OBE on the astral plane.

Reading this book will wash away your fears about astral travel and break barriers holding you back. You will also learn how to work with the energy around you, address challenges, and stay protected during your journey. Finally, you will know how to integrate your out-of-body experiences as a seasoned astral projector. Consider it your handy collection of time, space, and phases of your explorations into exotic higher dimensions.

In this comprehensive guide, you will learn how to forge your own unique path, better understand and accept yourself, and embrace your authenticity. You will find strength and peace in your energy. You will see that you don't need to fit into the cookie-cutter molds the earthly Matrix expects and demands of you. Astral projection can tell you about the world, yourself, and where you're going. As a result, you will see how easy it is to craft your own roadmap. Life is not a one-size-fits-all. It's a canvas you can paint however you wish.

The profound insights gained from OBEs are your gateway to personal and spiritual growth. This book is packed with benefits, such as emotional healing and creativity boosts. You'll come away with an encyclopedia of astral projection knowledge that will impact the rest of your life and improve the lives of those around you.

You'll discover how astral travel can rid you of anxiety once and for all as you discover your unconscious strengths and psychic abilities. Psychological breakthroughs you've tried to make will finally be possible through the exercises you engage in here.

Astral projection is a personal experience that differs for each individual. Some people become more spiritual after it, and some don't. However, everyone comes away with a newfound value for life, especially if their experience was successful. With this book, you can guarantee success and will gain the confidence to bravely plow ahead.

While many groups, cultures, religions, philosophies, and organizations can sometimes offer their insight as absolute truths, OBEs allow you to define what is true for yourself. You will determine your mythology with a guide tailored to your needs.

All you need is a little patience and practice. Astral projection will soon become a habit, and by the end of this book, you'll know how to consciously separate and return your astral body to your physical one with ease.

This book allows you to explore the unconscious positively and reap the benefits so that you develop a new attitude towards life and live with intention. So, start reading the ultimate guide to traveling outside your body, astral projection, and journeying beyond the Matrix.

Read on to unlock the key to your wildest dreams!

Chapter 1: The Matrix and How Astral Projection Can Help You Escape

Have you wondered why you can't realize your full potential? Why, no matter how hard you work or how much you pursue something, it's never enough? What if you are told this is because you live in a conditioned physical reality called the Matrix? This chapter explores the concept of this carefully constructed but all the more deceptive world. You will learn about the impact of the Matrix and how it keeps people confined and in painful ignorance. You will also learn about astral projection, one of the most powerful techniques of escaping the Matrix. This ancient method can help you break all the chains, opening your soul to new, enlightening experiences.

To escape the Matrix, you first need to have a comprehensive understanding of it.[1]

The Matrix Concept

The idea of the Matrix stems from a belief that people are constantly surrounded by limitations. While popular culture brought it into the limelight at the turn of the 20th century, this isn't a new concept. It's an ancient one that is present in many cultures and traditions worldwide.

Perhaps one of the ideologies closest to the beliefs surrounding the Matrix is *Gnosticism*. According to Gnostic teachings, the physical world could be perceived as a deceptive prison created by the Demiurge to trap souls in deliberate confusion. When people's souls enter the world surrounding them, they relinquish something fundamental. They lose the ability to govern their spirituality.

Except, the souls don't just lose their identity. It's stolen from them. By whom? The creator of the physical world, the *Demiurge*. Unlike creators from other spiritual beliefs, the Demiurge doesn't have pure intentions. He doesn't help the souls heighten and enlighten. Instead, he wants them to be consumed in a false reality. The Demiurge keeps people in ignorance because it allows him to control the souls.

How does the Demiurge get away with it? He uses distraction and manipulation. Even the basic needs become tools of distraction. These clever architects enhance every need, creating desires far beyond what individuals need. Yet, people become ensnared in a belief that they must satisfy their desires. The same goes for material possessions.

According to the Gnostic beliefs, all physical possessions in the world are objects of distractions. People continue pursuing success and validation, remaining chained to the idea of more. They live unfulfilled lives because nothing is ever enough. All these ideas are architectured by the Demiurge and perpetuated by every participant. The participants create societal contracts, pressures, and restraints – all of which act like a glue that binds the different ignorant and mistaken beliefs together.

The Modern Matrix Theory

While incorporating ancient beliefs (including Gnostic teachings), the modern Matrix theory also acknowledges the contemporary forms of falsities within the physical world. Never before has there been a time when people were as influenced by materialism and consumerism as they are in modern times. The massive amount of pressure and the vast number of sources of strain come from creating a seemingly indestructible form of oppression of the souls. You'll never realize your full potential when all you can see is what you must have, what you still need, and what you're missing from your life.

Do you know what else can hinder you from becoming the best version of yourself – the best version of your soul? Your subconscious desires. Like material needs, every other desire is carefully constructed to make you believe it is real. Even worse, you assume that is how it should be.

According to the modern Matrix theory, societal symbols are manipulated by people who are all trapped in the Matrix. No one is free except those who choose to liberate their souls by leaving through one means or another.

Some followers of the modern Matrix theory describe reality as a dream. People have subjective experiences in dreams, just like the false physical world that traps their souls. The only exception is that this dream isn't hiding in anyone's consciousness. It's out in the open. Have you ever had a dream about something you were sure already happened in real life? You just can't remember where and when you had this experience. You were left wondering what happened and what the dream could mean.

This often happens in the Matrix, too. People are left without answers after familiar experiences when, in fact, these events are likely related to their soul and its previous journey through life and the universe.

Astral Projection – Escaping the Matrix

As its name implies, astral projection means projecting into the astral world. What are you projecting? To put it simply, your soul. The soul that's trapped in the Matrix. Yes, you can escape those constraints that obscure your spiritual identity and keep you from realizing your full potential.

Through astral projection, your soul can leave your body and travel anywhere, anytime. For the same reason, astral projection causes what's called *"out-of-body experiences"* or OBEs. How can this method help you escape the Matrix? All those constraints from the Matrix affect the physical body. When your soul leaves the physical body, it can move freely. It doesn't know physical desires. It's not affected by the proximity or influence of material possessions. Even more importantly, your soul can move freely from any societal restrictions.

When you astral project, your soul travels to higher planes where none of the above exists. There is only spiritual wisdom to gather and no fears and limitations to hinder you. In these higher planes, your soul can reconnect with its core identity and explore its existence.

Astral Projection Across Cultures

Astral projection is a permanent fixture in several cultures. Since ancient times, shamans used various methods to enter a higher plane of existence. Some called this a *"soul flight,"* which coincides with the contemporary description of astral projection.

According to Shamanism, the world is divided into two parts. One of these is what people are consciously aware of, full of conditioning, patterns of beliefs, social norms, and adapted behaviors. The other part can only be reached by entering into a higher state of consciousness. Shamans enter into this state through journeying. This journey or soul flight is facilitated with a ritualistic practice of drumming, chanting, and, sometimes, consciousness-altering substances. The shaman's soul leaves the body to explore the higher state and access spiritual knowledge hidden from the conscious awareness.

Shamanic journey or soul flight often has the purpose of communicating or connecting with a deity. After entering an altered state of consciousness, shamans can form a profound connection with the deity of their choice and gain wisdom from them. This practice is often dedicated to either honoring a deity or asking them specific questions. It can be used as a form of divination, to gather strategic wisdom to defend or attack, and more.

In other Indigenous cultures, astral projection is called *"spirit walking"* and *"Sukshma Sharira."* According to these beliefs, entering the spiritual world can help you answer all your questions. Spirit walks are rituals through which religious practitioners visit the spiritual world, seeking answers to their inquiries. They can enter this world in a dream state or while awake but in an altered state of consciousness. By lulling themselves into a state that isn't tied to physical limitations, they allow their soul to "walk" through the divide between the physical and the spiritual world.

In Eastern beliefs, Sukshma Sharira is the subtle body, which permeates the physical body with vitality and energy. The physical body, Sthula Sharira, depends on the subtle body and is subject to the changes caused by the physical world. It's the same as the astral body, the form the soul takes on the astral plane. Sukshma Sharira can leave the physical body only when it is liberated from the confines of the physical reality.

Many believe people are closest to the Sukshma Sharira in the dream state because they are more connected to the subconscious than the conscious, which is controlled by the physical state. However, some cultures use practices to encourage the Sukshma Sharira to leave its restraints in an awakened but slightly altered state.

Exploring the Astral Plane

Wandering around the astral plane can help you liberate yourself from the confines of the Matrix, even when your soul returns. How? When you are on the astral plane, your actions must be intentional. You have to know where you are going and why you're going there. This has two benefits. It gives you direction, so you won't wander around aimlessly.

It also gives you power. In the Matrix, very few aspects of your life are in your control. On the astral plane, you are in charge of yourself. In the Matrix, you can't get answers to questions like "Is this real?" or "Am I living a true reality or a false imitation of what my soul is intended to achieve?" Exploring the astral plane can give you truthful answers to these questions.

On the astral plane, your soul knows what's real and what's an illusion. It senses reality because it's the closest to its true identity here. So, if something you discover here as truth differs from your physical life experience, you'll know that your physical reality is nothing but an imitation.

You can leave the ignorant state behind, lift the haze around you, and start living life to the fullest. You can see you're more than a being with physical needs and desires for material possessions. You can break free from all the societal, cultural, and habitual conditioning you've been subjected to in the physical world. You can pursue and achieve your full potential.

Intentional and Unintentional Out-of-Body Experiences

The out-of-body experiences you can achieve with astral projection are intentional. However, many people have similar experiences unintentionally, too. Some are spontaneous and can prompt sudden instances of realization that your physical existence in this world isn't the true reality. Others can appear due to traumatic events or circumstances where the body, mind, and soul endure severe stress. For example, some people can have out-of-body experiences during or after having surgery. Others can experience something similar when they are injured or witness someone close to them get hurt.

Astral projection allows you to have intentional out-of-body experiences.*

Near-death experiences are incredibly traumatic events that can cause people to feel like their soul has left their bodies for a few moments. The trauma and stress they endure compel them to separate from their baseline consciousness and step outside of it. This leads to the belief that they stepped outside themselves. In reality, they only left the state of consciousness they knew and wandered onto a different one.

Like near-death experiences, psychedelic-induced states can also prompt out-of-body experiences. However, these states are just as dangerous as stepping outside the body due to shocking events. Why? In either case, you have no control over your actions. Not only do you act unintentionally, but you can also put yourself in danger. You go in blind and have no way of navigating your journey. You can't defend yourself from negative influences, and, even more importantly, you may not be able to return safely.

In unintentional out-of-body experiences, people leave their bodies because they don't feel safe. While astral projection also requires you to exit your body, you should always feel safe in it. Otherwise, your return can become a stressful event.

By losing your power over your experience in a psychedelic-induced state, you also lose the sense of safety in your body. Though granting a sense of liberation, going through this experience can also be disempowering. A similar event can occur during illness-induced episodes. For example, people suffering from epilepsy, dissociative disorders, and severe anxiety can also experience the sense of leaving their body. They, too, feel unsafe, so they leave their body but feel powerless to control their return.

Lucid dreaming is a milder form of out-of-body experience. Unlike intentional astral projection, lucid dreaming allows you to retain a sense of control of your environment. You can interact with everything and everyone similarly to how you do in the physical reality. You can also navigate your actions and the actions of those around you. However, you may lose control of some of your senses. For example, your sense of smell may be dull, and your eyes may become unfocused. You may be unable to read because the part of your brain responsible for it is asleep.

During astral travel, your senses remain sharp, and you can read because your mind remains fully active. You aren't dreaming, and you are more conscious than ever before. You leave your body consciously and continue exploring your surroundings the same way. You won't control the entities around you, but they will interact with you. You are aware you aren't dreaming because you have an elevated sense of awareness of everything.

Without a doubt, astral travel is the safest way to explore out-of-body experiences. It's a spiritual practice that gives people greater awareness than many unintentional experiences, including near-death ones.

Intentional travel also poses a much lower risk because people don't feel as confined in their bodies. In psychedelic-induced experiences, the feeling of confinement can be extremely high, sometimes leading to a state of distress and unsafe returns. While the sense of confinement may be somewhat lower in other unintentional out-of-body experiences, it can still be disempowering enough to be unsafe.

Another unique characteristic of astral travel is that practitioners often lose their sense of time. Try as they might, those who enter the altered state of consciousness with the help of psychedelic substances can't let go of a sense of urgency. They're aware of the time passing because they're too tied to physical reality. What does this mean? It means they can't explore the higher state as freely as they would be able to with astral travel.

Astral travel can lead to a loss of the sense of time.[3]

With controlled, intentional astral travel, you set the intention to remain aware but unconfined. You send your consciousness outside your physical body, letting it freely travel and explore the astral realm. You may have an altered perception of the word, but feel safe. You can stay in your body, look down on yourself, or travel through time and space. You're free to choose what you want to do.

Wisdom from the Astral Plane

What wisdom can you uncover through astral projection? This may depend on your level of experience and spiritual needs. For example, some people have gained insight into their relationship with the spiritual world, spirit guides, or ancestral spirits. Others have revered exploring the higher planes of spiritual existence, where they can expand their souls' wisdom with knowledge far beyond what is available in the physical realm.

There were also those who, for the first time, experienced the liberating sensation of not being restricted by anything, physically, mentally, or spiritually. They've seen just how much constraints the physical world has put on them. They could visualize the differences between this world and the spiritual state they were exploring.

The wisdom you uncover in the astral realm can empower you to live your life more authentically and intentionally. It prompts you to free yourself from the chains of societal, cultural, and material constraints. It lets you take back control and gain ownership of every part of your life, including the spiritual one.

Your spiritual self craves to reconnect with its true identity. This higher identity is very empowering. It's also a source of guidance for a more authentic life. Through astral travel, you can rediscover it and rebuild your bond with it, so you can always tap into its power when you need a boost of strength and confidence to combat the falsities of the Matrix.

Besides granting you agency over your spirituality, intentional out-of-body experiences like astral travel have plenty of other benefits. Just like their predecessors, modern practitioners also use astral travel to explore and gain a profound understanding of nature, the universe, the deities they follow, and people's place amid everything else. You can connect to the world around you, and not just the spiritual planes. You can find guidance, answers to questions, and much more. You can find your true purpose within the world. Living without purpose stifles spiritual growth. Unfortunately, living in the Matrix doesn't leave much room for finding your purpose. Through astral travel, you can discover what you're truly meant to do, what the universe has intended for you, and what brings fulfillment to your soul.

Living in the Matrix comes with insecurities, confusion, and fear of not fitting in or not being good enough. These limitations can hold you back from achieving your full potential. Through astral projection, you can see how much you're capable of, prompting you to overcome these self-limiting apprehensions. It shows you that what matters is what you can do, not what you can't. It doesn't matter if what you can do goes against the societal norms for fitting in. These likely aren't based on your values. While exploring the astral realm, you can gather courage and transform into a more confident version of yourself.

By liberating yourself from the physical ties to your body, astral travel will open up a realm of possibilities. When you feel like you need to escape the physical world's limitations, you'll be able to do it safely and travel wherever you don't feel as restricted. You can have experiences you never had before (because you've felt trapped by the physical world). These experiences can enrich your life in a meaningful way, bringing you fulfillment and joy every step of the way.

Suppose you experienced an unintentional out-of-body experience (for example, during a traumatic event) before, and this left you scared of similar circumstances. In that case, astral travel can alleviate your fears. By staying in control when leaving your body, you can show yourself that what happened to you is a normal experience and you have nothing to be fearful of. You'll learn to let go because you'll always be in control.

Astral travel may also empower psychic and spiritual-seeking abilities. It encourages you to practice visualization, grounding, and other techniques necessary for gathering and deciphering spiritual knowledge. The more you practice these during your travels, the stronger they become.

Chapter 2: The Quantum Science of Out-of-Body Experiences

Now that you know that out-of-body experiences rely on a higher level of awareness, which prompts a different form of consciousness, you may be interested in learning more about how that consciousness forms. This chapter explores the scientific background of out-of-body experiences, combining them with their spiritual significance and providing a more well-rounded picture of how these events occur.

By examining the neurological, psychological, and metaphysical phenomena involved in out-of-body experiences, this chapter will help you understand what consciousness is. It will also highlight specific structures involved in raising awareness.

After the theoretical introduction, this chapter will provide several practical techniques for enhancing awareness, including wavelength training, body scans, and frequency alignment through sound vibrations.

The Neurological Basis of OBEs

Scientific evidence suggests that out-of-body experiences have a neurological background. Scientists have confirmed that these events can occur during sleep, hypnosis, anesthesia, and illnesses (Muldoon, 2013). Their theories were backed by questionnaire studies, where a group of selected individuals described moments when they felt like they had moved out of their bodies (Blackmore S.J., 1982).

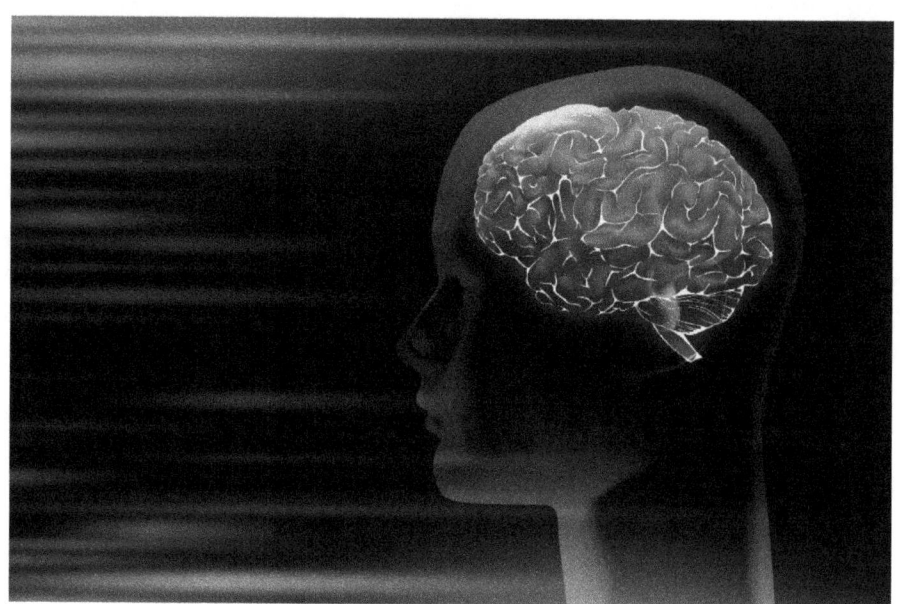
It's thought that out-of-body experiences have a neurological background.'

Researchers have found a connection between migraines and out-of-body experiences, too. This evidence was crucial to finding the key regions associated with these events. Based on this, scientists have linked out-of-body experiences to neural regions responsible for multisensory, vestibular, and visual processing. Multisensory processing refers to the information processing through all the senses. They're the most affected regions during out-of-body experiences.

The neural regions responsible for multisensory processing have a similar anatomical and functional distribution to the regions controlling vestibular processing. The latter refers to experiences related to the perception of movement and size of the body and limbs. Scientists have found that the electrical stimulation of the multisensory and vestibular areas can lead to the same consequences as events leading to spontaneous out-of-body experiences (Blanke et al., 2002). Namely, when stimulating the vestibular region, people experience the sensation of elevation and lightness or perceive the rotation of the body, which does not actually occur in the physical body. Or, they see and feel their limbs move without moving the actual physical limb.

More recent research confirmed that out-of-body experiences most often occur during the REM sleep stage (Campillo-Ferrer et al., 2024). During this phase, people can also experience sleep paralysis, which means they cannot move due to altered brain activity. Sleep paralysis usually occurs right after the first cycle of REM sleep begins, followed by lucid dreaming or a feeling of stepping outside the body. Sometimes, the two occurrences overlap, and people experience sleep paralysis and an out-of-body state simultaneously. Observed individuals who reported frequent out-of-body experiences while falling asleep also show a short first REM cycle and neural activity that mimics both a state of REM sleep and wakefulness (Raduga et al., 2020).

Out-of-body experiences occur during the REM stage of sleep.[5]

Psychedelic substances can also lead to a changed neurological state where a person may have out-of-body experiences. Some lead to a state of relaxation and/or heightened senses, where a person can focus more on grounding themselves (or do it unintentionally) and leaving their physical body. Other psychedelics cause a lack of functional connectivity in neural pathways (Carhart-Harris, 2018). A third group contains a substance called DMT (N, N-dimethyltryptamine), which also prompts neurological processes that lead to self-dissolution.

The changes related to out-of-body experiences happen on several fronts. One is the disintegration between the person's extrapersonal and personal space. In other words, the person can't distinguish where their own personal space ends and where their surroundings begin. This leads to them perceiving themselves differently in their interpersonal space (i.e., they see themselves in a different place than where they are). This occurs because the neurological pathways are blocked between the brain's temporal and parietal regions (Blanke, 2004). This brain connection is responsible for providing the proper perception of space.

The second neurological change that leads to out-of-body experiences is the disintegration within the personal space. This indicates that a person's senses are confused about their own perception. Thus, people can see themselves from outside their bodies instead of perceiving themselves as a whole(Blanke, 2004).

A crucial structure that may hold the answer to the question of why out-of-body experiences occur is the pineal gland. In many cultures, the pineal gland is seen as the seat of the soul or the third eye. The pineal gland is an endocrine gland set in the middle of the two brain hemispheres and is known to secrete the hormone melatonin. Melatonin is responsible for maintaining a healthy circadian rhythm (day and night functions). It's what makes you sleepy at night and wake up in the morning when the sun comes up. The circadian rhythm is closely connected to the day/night cycle, and so is the production of melatonin. Moreover, melatonin is derived from the feel-good hormone serotonin, leading to a subject-causal relationship between a positive state of mind and out-of-body experiences. How? When you have a healthy circadian rhythm, you produce more serotonin. In turn, more serotonin turns into more melatonin, leading to more frequent and productive out-of-body experiences.

Some researchers suggested that the pineal gland also produces a DMT, the substance that leads to a heightened state of awareness and out-of-body experiences. The gland secretes the molecule in small amounts, but the amount may be increased during stressful events, including near-death experiences (StJohn, 2017). This supports the belief that the pineal gland (or third eye) is a link to spiritual enlightenment and improved spiritual practices.

Practitioners have developed various methods for opening, activating, or bringing awareness to the pineal gland, and for a good reason. When fully activated, it helps reach a higher state of consciousness and an intuitive understanding of everything in the universe (including all realms and planes).

How do the practices of activating the pineal gland work? One explanation is that they boost melatonin production. Higher melatonin production is associated with an altered state of consciousness, just as it is with nighttime. In other words, when you go to sleep (and dream), your pineal gland produces more melatonin. As you remember, spontaneous out-of-body experiences often occur at the beginning of sleep. This is likely due to the increased melatonin production at this time. Through meditation, visualization, and breathing practices, you can achieve the same effect and prompt your pineal gland to help propel you into an out-of-body experience while awake.

Melatonin and DMT are crucial in shifting your body to an altered state of consciousness, whether during sleep or when awake. They both facilitate a shift of consciousness, which can lead to spiritual and immersive experiences outside your physical body.

Quantum Theories of Consciousness

As helpful as observing the neurological basis of out-of-body experiences is, some of their aspects can't be explained through neurological connections. To fill in the gaps, scientists have coined the term quantum consciousness. It refers to non-localized effects (effects transpiring outside the body) of non-neurological phenomena that affect the brain cells. These effects can alter brain functions and can shed light on how consciousness works.

Observations of people with near-death experiences have confirmed that disembodiment (separation from the body) occurs due to non-local consciousness (Greyson, 2006).

You might wonder what prompts this non-local consciousness and awareness. The answer could lie in the quantum theories of consciousness. According to one of these theories, conscious experiences are induced by vibrations. The human body receives energy, information, and matter through vibrations. These vibrations come from a vibrational field surrounding the body. This field can carry, send, and receive vibrations and everything they transmit. It can be accessed by the body's own energy field. Connecting to and receiving vibrations can provide an explanation as to how out-of-body experiences occur.

Where do quantum theories of consciousness stem from? *From quantum mechanics.*

According to this discipline, matter can only be observed if broken down to energy. Everything moves as the energy moves. In fact, matter could only exist because something makes the energy move. This something is a force powerful enough to cause energy shifts, which are known as vibrations.

Everything emits vibrations, including humans. Likewise, everything and everyone can manipulate the vibrations around them, too. This is a unique ability – which, in humans, is linked to consciousness. According to scientists, including Max Planck (the father of modern quantum physics), matter comes from consciousness, and it is why everyone can manipulate matter.

The vibrational state is a crucial element in out-of-body experiences and astral projection. The role of the vibrational state is highlighted in both the scientific principles of frequency and energy and esoteric teachings in which astral travel is practiced.

What is the vibrational state? It's best described as a humming or buzzing feeling that travels all across your body. This sensation is caused by the powerful vibrations coursing through your body. When you reach the vibrational state, you can start separating your body from your consciousness.

In the past, scientists believed that consciousness is formed in the brain. However, more and more evidence suggests that consciousness exists beyond the brain. Besides science, observations in spiritual communities also support the idea of non-local (or out-of-brain) consciousness. Spiritual literature and philosophical texts are punctuated with descriptions of individuals who observed themselves from above while having their eyes closed or transferred to remote locations without their bodies moving. In some cultures, the practice and experiences of leaving the body have been woven into symbols. These symbols are used for guidance and protection during out-of-body experiences or other spiritual practices that require spiritual (astral) travel.

The modern science of *thanatology*, which studies death, has seen similar observations. People near death reported traveling to remote locations or hovering above their bodies, preparing for the next stage in life. All this suggests that consciousness may reside in other locations instead of in the brain, most likely in a field that can be accessed by a higher state of awareness.

The basic premise of astral travel is that consciousness separates itself from the body – not just the brain. As a physical component of a person, the psychological body is closely connected to the non-physical component, the soul. The brain is also a physical complement, while consciousness is a non-physical component. The connection between all these components is held up by the mind.

The physical and non-physical components function separately in many belief systems and practices. For example, the soul and the consciousness are separate from the brain and body. Yet, the mind still acts like a bridge, granting control over all parts, including the ones that live separately, like the consciousness. In these cultures, where the soul is believed to live separately, it is also a commonly accepted fact that the soul can leave the body and connect to the consciousness, whether it's during a spiritual practice or after the decay and passing of the physical body.

Psychologists define consciousness as an awareness of an individual's experiences. Your consciousness incorporates past and current thoughts, feelings, and perceptions of your surroundings, others, and situations. Your consciousness determines how you will perceive everything that makes it up and how you define everything to yourself. It's a unique collection of everything you bring into your awareness and how you relate to everything.

Each state of consciousness controls your awareness of everything you pick up from your environment, thoughts, feelings, and actions. In other words, depending on your consciousness state, you will perceive conscious awareness differently.

Consciousness affects your priorities, decisions, resilience, learning, and many other abilities. Many of these skills play fundamental roles in out-of-body experiences and astral travel. Understanding how to tap into the right state of consciousness to perpetuate awareness of the right factors/situations/ thoughts/feelings, etc., is crucial for a successful astral journeying practice.

The Hermetic Principle of Vibration, stemming from the esoteric teaching of Hermeticism, states that even feelings and thoughts have vibrations, not just the energy that prompts them. Just as the energy remains in constant motion, so do the thoughts and feelings through their vibrations. By tuning into the frequencies of your thoughts and feelings, you gain more insight and control over them. This can enrich spiritual practices like astral travel and lead to overall spiritual growth.

The law of attraction is another ideology of esoteric origins. According to this law, a person's vibrational frequency determines what frequencies they will attract. How does this work? Everything you link to your consciousness becomes energy. This energy vibrates at a certain frequency, which attracts everything that vibrates at the same frequency.

In other words, by focusing on something that vibrates at a specific frequency and pushing it into your consciousness, you can attract and bring it into your life. If you push positive thoughts into your consciousness, these will become positive energy. Guess what this energy will attract? More positive energy. On the other hand, if you fill your consciousness with negativity, you will only bring more negativity to your life.

While the two previous esoteric principles attest to the likelihood of consciousness residing outside the brain (as this is the only way it can interact with energy and vibrations), scientists have found even more evidence to support this. Namely, psychologists have determined that every individual depends on their surroundings to form the unique collection that makes up their consciousness. Why? The brain likes to delegate tasks to occupy itself with more important processes. Anything that isn't deemed a primary concern is sent to automatic information processing tools. These tools are based on outside experiences and perceptions of the environment. The brain constantly builds a new mechanism for processing – this is called neuroplasticity. Some tools are physical – for example, the brain learns when you take an object to perform a task. It stores the information on how you used the object, and the next time you use it, your brain automatically signals the correct steps for using the object. The same applies to non-physical tools, too. Spiritual tools can just as easily become an extension of your brain as physical tools. Remember, a powerful connection exists between a person's physical and non-physical parts. This helps create links to other non-physical entities, too.

Your brain has a flexible perception of both your physical body and energy. It's connected to both, and because they're both in constant motion due to the energy shifts within them, the brain sees them as fluid entities and not fixed states. It connects the inside and the outside and provides an opportunity for the energy to course freely between the two spaces. The more the physical and non-physical parts of yourself can interact, the more unified they will become. Whether you interact with your environment physically (through touch or other senses) or spiritually (by reaching out to your consciousness), you're creating contexts for your brain to process and interpret. The more you interact with your consciousness, the more aware you'll be of its connection and its seclusion from the brain.

Brainwave Awareness Meditation

Meditation can alter the frequency of your brain vibrations, otherwise known as brain waves. How? Meditation is a practice that promotes slowing down and being in the present. It forces you to calm your body and mind so your mind can't wander toward unhelpful or negative thoughts. The more relaxed you become and the less your mind can roam off, the more it affects your brain waves.

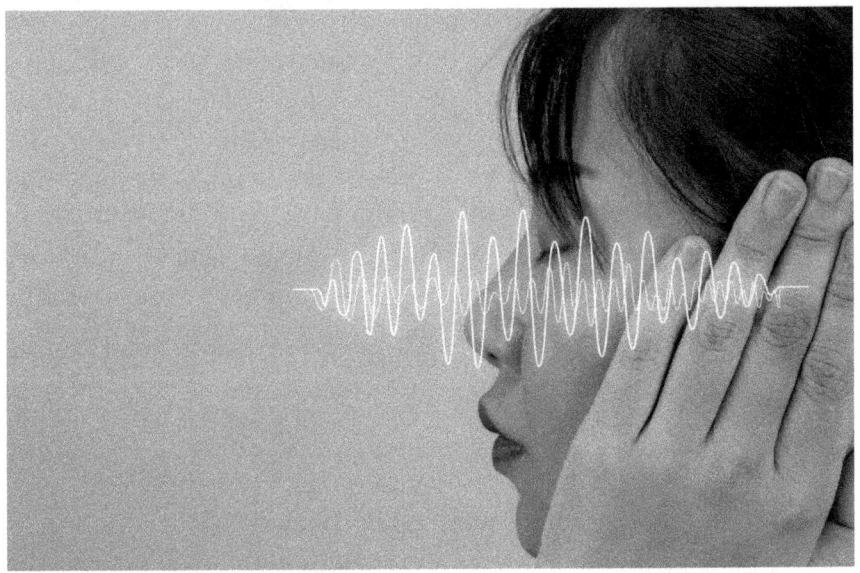

Brainwaves are indications of different levels of activity.[6]

Brain waves indicate a level of activity. Depending on the activity, your brain emits waves of different wavelengths:

- **Delta Waves:** Indicate the slowest function and lowest awareness.
- **Theta Waves:** Still slow but higher awareness, especially towards consciousness.
- **Alpha Waves:** Indicate a relaxed but alert brain.
- **Beta Waves:** A sign of an alert brain, ready to process information.
- **Gamma Waves:** Emitted during the highest levels of alertness and focus.

With the following meditation technique, you can tune into your brainwaves and alter them to have richer out-of-body experiences.

Instructions:
1. Choose a quiet, comfortable space where you won't be disturbed.
2. Get comfortable, either by sitting or lying down.
3. Close your eyes and take a slow, deep breath.
4. Release your breath equally slowly, repeat, and continue taking deep breaths until you relax.
5. Focus on the air filling your lungs as you take each deep breath. When you exhale, notice how the air leaves your body, leaving your lungs deflated.
6. As you focus on this repeated pattern of full emptiness, notice your thoughts. Do you still have a good bit of mental chatter clouding your mind? If so, continue breathing and relaxing.
7. Keep going until you notice that your mental activity quiets down. Imagine that your breathing acts like a dimmer switch for a light. The more you focus on it, the dimmer the light – or, in this case, the mental activity – becomes.
8. Notice the stillness in your brain. Revel in it. Your brain is relaxed, emitting alpha or theta waves. If you're feeling sleepy, it may be alpha. You've eased into theta waves if your brain feels relaxed, but your inner awareness is high.
9. Remain in the stillness for 10-15 minutes. Enjoy this moment, and know it will bring you closer to your spiritual goals.
10. For the best results, practice this meditation daily for 10-15 minutes. You can choose the time of day most convenient for you. What matters most is that you dedicate time and effort to notice those moments of stillness.

Body Scan to Increase Pineal Gland Awareness

As a powerful awareness-enhancing tool, the third eye (pineal gland) can facilitate out-of-body experiences, granting safe travel and return. However, do you remember that the pineal gland only secretes the awareness-enhancing molecule in larger quantities at certain times? If you want it to assist you in reaching a higher state of consciousness and traveling outside your physical body, you must activate your pineal gland first.

By activating it, you bring awareness to the pineal gland. As a result, you'll have increased creativity, deeper intuition, and a stronger connection between your spirituality and its true identity.

The following exercise increases pineal gland awareness. It's a twist on the classic body scan technique where practitioners gradually become aware of the various sensations they feel in their bodies.

Instructions:
1. Find a dark and quiet room where you won't be disturbed.
2. Place a mat or blanket on the floor and lie down.
3. When you feel comfortable, close your eyes.
4. Take a deep breath through your nose and inhale through your mouth.
5. Continue breathing deeply, raising your awareness of your body with every breath you take.
6. Imagine you feel a deeper level of relaxation. Imagine you're sinking deeper into relaxation.
7. With each breath, focus on your chest and shoulders rising and falling.
8. Then, imagine a warm, glowing light appearing on your toes. In your mind, see this light slowly creep up toward your legs, hips, back, and all the way to your head.
9. When the light reaches your forehead (right between your eyes, where your pineal gland lies), imagine it permeating inside your brain. See the red, warm glow deep inside, illuminating your pineal gland.
10. Continue breathing deeply and see the light growing brighter with each breath.
11. Focus on seeing the light within your brain until it feels comfortable.
12. Repeat the scan regularly. Your awareness of the light (and your pineal gland) will increase with each repetition. Your focus will become sharper until you intuitively see where the light travels and when it reaches your pineal gland. You also become more aware of the pineal gland and whether it's active in helping you achieve better spiritual experiences.

Frequency Alignment with Sound

Brain waves can be altered via any vibration, including music and sounds. The brainwaves match the frequency of the sound's vibrations. Matching your brain waves to certain sounds reduces stress, enriches meditation efforts, and promotes emotional and spiritual release.

Binaural beats are the most frequently used frequencies for brain wave alignment. Incorporating two different frequencies, these beats trick the brain into perceiving a third frequency. The brain adopts this third frequency, which is often a theta wave. Reaching the theta wave, the brain can relax and have increased awareness of consciousness and the inner self.

Instructions:

1. Find a quiet and comfortable place where you won't be disturbed. To be able to fully take advantage of the benefits of binaural beats (and ensure you won't be disrupted), use headphones.
2. Prepare a binaural beat soundtrack.
3. Sit or lie down in a comfortable position.
4. Close your eyes and take a few deep breaths.
5. Then, imagine feeling the sound waves. They aren't just in your ears. They have entered your head and are slowly traveling through your body.
6. Notice how the sound waves make you feel. You may feel warmth or a tingling sensation. It may be a foreign feeling – but try to relax. The more you relax, the more subtle sensations you will be able to pick up.
7. Continue relaxing and breathing deeply as the soundwaves travel through your body for 10 minutes.
8. After 10 minutes, return your breathing to normal and stop the soundtrack. Can you still notice some sensations? This is normal. You're in a higher vibrational state.
9. Your vibrational state will diminish over time, so practicing this daily is crucial. Remember, you must be in a higher vibrational state to have a successful out-of-body experience. By practicing diligently, you can keep yourself in this state for longer.

Chapter 3: Preparing for a Journey Beyond the Body

A successful trip to the astral plane doesn't just happen. It requires mental and physical preparation. People tend to have high expectations and fears regarding astral travel – as if there's some big secret to successfully journeying beyond the body. However, the truth is that it's all about practice and patience. The habits that help you achieve an out-of-body experience are ones you should incorporate, regardless of whether they improve your quality of life in the physical world as much as they do in the spiritual realms.

There are a number of things you can do to prepare yourself for astral travel.[7]

This chapter will teach you how to create the ideal conditions for a successful OBE. You will know exactly how to align your mental, physical, and emotional well-being and ignite your consciousness with skills to enter a relaxed, focused state conducive to successful astral projection.

Ideal Conditions for an Intentional OBE

A Calm and Distraction-Free Environment

To put yourself in the right headspace, you need to create a calm, comfortable environment. Find somewhere comfortable to sit or lie down. Imagine this space filled with a protective light swirling all around you and every time you enter it, you feel the vibrations of this magic light attracting heavenly angels to guide you. This space is where you must practice your meditation and projection techniques, so you need to feel good about it. It should feel safe and secure. You want to feel the warm sensation of higher dimensions magnetizing your liberated soul.

Wear loose clothing and make sure there are no interruptions or interferences. Put your phone away and turn your alarm off. Distractions make it hard to stay grounded in the energy you hope to embrace. This can lead to doubt and insecurities, making it harder to prepare for handling unplanned situations and encounters in the astral realm. The goal is to prepare your mind and body for the condition you want to be in so you can remember what that feels like if it's ever challenged in the spiritual world.

Most people have their preferences regarding setting the ideal tone for a relaxing atmosphere. Some use protective symbols like crystals to maintain the energy they want in the room with them. Others focus on tools for relaxation, such as scents and sounds. They play soothing music and use essential oils like lavender to help them get in a relaxed mood.

Some people like to use crystals as they are believed to clear the surrounding energy.[8]

A Healthy Diet and Lifestyle

Diet and lifestyle choices can have positive and negative effects on your physical health, which, in turn, affects your mental health since food alters your energy. Healthy foods like leafy green vegetables have a positive influence, bringing out a positive essence. Unhealthy foods, particularly sugary drinks and snacks, can be detrimental to your body, creating a negative essence.

You want your body to function at a higher and lighter vibration, so you must eat foods that give you good energy. You may notice that junk food can drain your energy, leading to functioning with a lower frequency than you would if you had a healthier diet. A nutritious diet leads to a higher frequency.

Foods that influence astral travel success are those with all the nutrients your body needs to energize and refuel. Stock your refrigerator and pantry with plenty of fruits and vegetables, especially hydrating greens like spinach and lettuce. Those are positive essence foods, also known as spirit foods, that regular astral travelers eat because they have the highest vibratory rate and provide you with an abundance of positive energy. If you have a sweet tooth, now is the time to cut down on sweets. You should also reduce caffeine as much as possible, as it can mess with your energy's natural vibration, resulting in an anxious and agitated energy, which won't help you stay calm and centered during your OBE.

Hydration massively impacts your ability to astral project. Water flushes toxins and waste from the body, removing many of those low vibratory rate foods mentioned above. So, if you have a cheat day, staying hydrated releases the unwanted substances your body stores to maintain healthy energy.

Adapt to a healthy eating routine for a week, and you'll notice a change in your mental and physical health. Consider it your spiritual diet. It should consist of reducing your consumption of negatively charged foods and instead consuming positive essence foods so you're well-prepared to begin your astral journey. By following a healthy diet, your body is recharged with a high vibratory rate of positive energy and ready to attempt astral travel.

A Positive Mindset

Without a positive mindset, your spiritual body is tainted by lingering feelings of doubt, which poisons your mind and ultimately affects your ability to astral project and enjoy other realms.

You must learn to foster a sense of safety and openness free from fear. An open, inviting, and uplifting aura diminishes doubt, which can mentally cripple you and derail your spiritual adventure. A positive mindset has profound physical impacts on your life experiences, so it should come as no surprise that it improves your astral travels. When positive energy flows through you, your body feels like it's vibrating and floating, and this is exactly what you're going for in an OBE.

Positive affirmations and energy work are the best ways to tap into a positive mindset. These will strengthen your mental well-being, lighten your energy to vibrate at a high frequency, and maintain that energy balance. You want to transfer positive energy from your physical body to your astral body, so start by imagining how you want to feel.

Affirm and repeat positive feelings every morning, speaking softly and calmly. You will not feel like you have to force yourself to be positive. Your brain will fully believe what you tell it, and then your body will feel lighter. That is key because if your body feels safe, your astral body will, too.

Once you have set the tone for the day, the progression of your positivity will be felt in your body, and your energy will adapt. It'll be easier to get rid of the tension in your body and doubts in your mind. Your natural vibratory state will become muscle memory, so your energy is in a state of readiness for your psychic journey.

Preparing Your Mind and Body for Astral Projection

A Consistent Daily Practice Routine

You need a consistent routine to develop mental focus and relaxation skills. Just ten to fifteen minutes a day can do wonders for your astral self. What you choose to incorporate in your spiritual practice must be something you can do regularly. As with most routines, the hardest part is sticking to it. Make sure you pick times suitable for your schedule and that you're well-rested before

Use the cozy environment you created as your practice area so that the minute you step into your safe space, you have everything you need to get into the right state of mind. To remain consistent, put a reminder on your phone and set up all you need for visualization and meditation. For meditation, you need tools for relaxation, such as protective symbols, crystals, etc., and for visualization, you need focus. So, eat foods that improve your cognitive abilities. Remember, no sugar!

Your routine shouldn't just consist of preparation in the practice area. Instead, it is everything leading up to practice. Good habits to incorporate are morning walks, healthy foods, hydration, and rest - stress will make it harder to focus. Always schedule practice at a time when you feel most relaxed. Morning people may prefer to schedule practice after breakfast, whereas night owls may find themselves most at peace before bed. Your practice ritual needs to suit your mental and physical needs. That way, you can guarantee you won't skip some days.

Calming Breathing Techniques

Breathing techniques are vital in calming the mind and preparing the body for altered states of consciousness. Deep breathing is a technique used in many meditation and yoga exercises because it's a natural and easy way to release mental stress and tension in the body. Focusing on breath flow allows you to connect to your body in ways that will benefit you both when preparing for your spiritual adventure and in the astral plane.

Breathing techniques allow you to be centered and recharge your energy.⁹

Breathwork recharges your energy and helps you tune into the moment. It allows you to determine your energetic space and take control of your thoughts, emotions, and reactions. The role of proper breathing techniques is to reset your mental and physical state and make you more aware of your consciousness when leaving the Matrix.

Breathwork is how you prepare, determine, and control your energy and is a major part of out-of-body experience training. When you draw breath in, you absorb energy from the universe, allowing you to reach a high vibratory rate. You breathe in energy, which circulates through your body and recharges your organs, resetting your nervous system. When you breathe out, you expel energy that keeps you on edge. Trapped energy looks like a clouded mind and an agitated body, making you feel drained and hopeless.

To combat this, understand what breathwork does and take time out of your day to practice mindful breathing. Use this simple guide to help you calm down in astral projection training:

1. Your first inhale is you drawing in inspiration and energy support. Your first breath out is releasing fear and stress you've been holding onto or unknowingly held within for a long time.
2. Your next inhale is you inhaling joy and peace and then exhaling discouragement and impatience.
3. Your third inhale is breathing in confidence and releasing doubt with your third exhale.
4. Your fourth and final deep breath gives you focus as you breathe out the remaining mental distractions and attention blockers. Repeat this process twice or four times until you feel relaxed and centered.

Calming breathing techniques are a powerful tool in helping your body feel lighter so you can raise your vibrations. It creates the positive essence needed to flow through your body. Always focus on your breath during practice and imagine it reaching the most tense areas. Hold the air in for at least four counts. The longer you hold onto it, the more positive energy you store, but do this reasonably to avoid holding your breath for too long and causing even more tension. With each practice, you'll notice yourself vibrating higher and for much longer, a skill you want during astral travel.

Start your calm breathing practice when you first wake up in the morning. Use this method during tasks that require physical energy and can lead to mental exertion. Those are the perfect times to start training your mind and body for any case scenario.

Suppose you find yourself rushing, and your mind starts drifting too far into the future, worrying about what you have to do, or you start pacing around, panicking and overwhelmed during the day. In that case, it's time to stop and practice your breathwork until you feel your nervous system shift, your body relax, and your mind settle down. Then, do another breathing round in the evening before you sleep. Fill your lungs so you can feel air deep in your chest, let it sit for a minute as you mentally count, and then expel it. Repeat until you feel your mind emptying of the day's mental clutter and tense muscles relaxing. Now, you'll know what to do if similar feelings take hold of you during an OBE.

When you're ready to use your breathing techniques to explore the astral realm, make sure you're in your calm environment, have your tools and guides, and speak your affirmations beforehand. Calm breathing will become second nature to you. With it, you can tune into the spiritual realm, maintain your sense of calm, and prevent your body from tightening in fear as you venture into the unknown.

Breathing will continue to make you feel alive in moments when you might feel the urge to cower in fear. This will help when you need to take control if you encounter negative entities during an OBE. Breathing carries life into your nose and through your body. It's your present self taking inspired action, bringing you closer to your future self's goal of temporarily leaving your physical body.

Clear Intentions and Purpose

Setting clear intentions before practice directs your astral travel experience where you want it to go. It allows you to clarify your purpose and decide what your intentions are.

When attempting an OBE for the first time, you'll likely have feelings of uncertainty. That is perfectly valid. That's why you must prepare yourself for the journey.

People assume that speaking with intention is just positive thinking, but that alone isn't enough. You'll still find yourself crippled with doubt from time to time if you only rely on that. Speaking your intentions aloud daily is getting your mind and body to truly believe in what you're saying. These aren't thoughts. This is your reality – you are defining your purpose.

Consider the practice of intention setting as meditation. You will write down your purpose for each practice, for instance: *"During this practice,*

I will focus on imagining myself floating out of my body," or *"For this practice, I will conquer my fear by reframing my emotions."* Keep your purpose in mind as you practice.

During practice is not the only time to focus on intentions. Make a list of positive affirmations to speak out loud morning and night to set your mood. People learn through repetition from childhood, so repeating your intentions will make it real to you.

Write down your intentions and affirmations and post them on a mirror or wall. As you say them out loud, your purpose will become clearer and more believable to you. You can use the following purposeful affirmations and even add some of your own as you become more acquainted with your needs:

- I am becoming aware of my potential.
- I am aware of my energy and can fine-tune it to suit my needs.
- There is an abundance of positive experiences awaiting me.
- I am entering a space of pure potential.
- I am ready to enter a realm of possibilities.
- I will connect with the quantum realm.
- I will enjoy my out-of-body experience.
- I can leave and return to my astral and physical bodies.
- I am strongly connected to my astral body, and my journey will be a success.

One way to help your body accept the words you're saying is to imagine a white light surrounding you as you speak your intention. This white light encircles you and absorbs your words. It surrounds you throughout the day and protects you like a shield when you're in bed at night. It keeps your affirmations alive and is a measure of your energy. It prevents doubts and negativity from disturbing you and attracts positive entities toward you, such as your spirit guides and ancestors. This way, you'll know you can always ask for support when you need it through meditation and will know to use this same method when on the astral plane.

Only with clear intentions can you program your mind for optimal success. With breathwork, visualization, and repetitive affirmations, you can alter your energy. As you reveal your intention, your mind will believe what you're saying, and your energy will make it true. You will feel warm whenever you verbalize your purpose. That is your energy adapting to your new reality.

Journaling

Journaling has been used forever to document experiences. It has helped people psychologically in overcoming issues and making progress on their mental health journeys. The concept of journaling can be your preparatory tool in astral projection. You can clarify your goals, document your experiences during practices, and list all the details of your journey to identify the progress you made over time.

Journaling gives another dimension to the gravity of your thoughts.[10]

Writing things down is a way to soak up all the important information you gather. It keeps your goals and triumphs in your heart so you can bask in the opportunities, growth, and experiences that bring you a sense of gratitude. Jotting challenges and setbacks down is also helpful because it allows you to overcome the struggles that hold you back emotionally.

Journaling also exercises your imagination and creativity as you plan what you hope to explore, a skill to nurture for OBEs. You can write about how floating outside your body might feel and what you expect to see when your physical body remains below. You can add notes that will help you in practice sessions, such as details of the image, so you can stay connected to it.

This will help you determine your reality and what you want to experience. You can even turn it into a short story to prepare for your desired outcome. Moreover, journal tips and solutions to motivate yourself on the more challenging days. Setbacks are normal, and writing about them allows you to recognize your energy. That is the first step in improving your energy and opening yourself up to your potential and possibilities. Then, you can continue to use journaling to remain positive and work on areas that need more assistance. For example, if you aren't getting quite where you want to go during practice, you can write down your concerns and doubts and then list ways to combat them and be more successful next time.

Prepare for your adventures by reflecting on what you've learned and tracking your growth and progress, deepening your spiritual connection. This will guide your future self in your future attempts. Write down ways to connect with your astral body, your observations during a session, aspects of meditation that inspired or even surprised you, your current goals and perspectives, and whether they have changed. This documentation is your key to aligning yourself with the energy you need for a positive OBE. Integrate all this information in your trials to provide yourself with steps that bring you closer to your goals. Consider your journal your book of meditative lessons.

Remember to give yourself time, and don't rush the process. There is a natural learning curve involved. So, rest assured, there is no time frame to adhere to. Some people have an OBE on their first try, while others need more time to prepare their mind and body. Remember that stress can interfere with motivation, so be reasonable when you set your expectations. There is no need to beat the clock to astral projection. The key qualities for success are patience and persistence, and even they only work when your mind and body are at ease and your energy is organized. You will then be able to look back at your journey through your writing and see every step forward and backward and every challenge, experience, and success that led you to this moment.

Practical Exercises

Breathing for Calm and Focus:

1. To practice deep, diaphragmatic breathing, use a combination of long breathing and breath-holding techniques. Make sure you're in a comfortable position. Close your eyes if it helps.
2. First, inhale through your nose for six counts and expel air through your mouth for another six.
3. Then, softly breathe in for four counts through your nose, hold for four counts, and breathe out through your mouth for six counts.

4. The third deep breath is the same, but on the exhale, close your eyes and make an "Oh" or "Ahh" shape with your mouth. You can even make a sound as you breathe out.
5. The fourth and final breath is a four-count inhale through your nose, followed by a four-count exhale through the mouth.
6. Repeat until you feel calm and focused.

Setting Clear Intentions:
1. Enter your practice area with your meditative tools and journal, and find a comfortable sitting or lying position.
2. Set a specific intention for today's session (for instance: "Today, I will explore a deeper state of relaxation" or "I will overcome doubts and obstacles") and write it in your journal.
3. Now, say it out loud, focusing on your simple and clear purpose for the day.
4. Repeat it silently during your practice session, especially when your mind drifts off.

Journaling for Preparation:
1. Begin a journal dedicated to your OBE journey and use it to clarify your goals, such as understanding a specific concept like breathwork or exploring a personal question, for example: "What fear is holding me back during practice?"
2. Through writing, explore the possible answers to your questions and determine the lessons of your next session, adding details that help you progress, such as a list of ways to improve the aspects you struggled with during the last practice round. (For example: "I will stay hydrated and eat well to improve my focus this time" or "I will add relaxing essential oils to avoid fixating on fears next time."
3. Write about your emotions, thoughts, and expectations before and after each session to track your progress and build confidence as you prepare for astral projection.

Chapter 4: Your First OBE on the Astral Plane

The time has come for your first attempts at an out-of-body experience. You've learned about the benefits of leaving the Matrix and how to prepare yourself and your space for leaving it. This chapter will continue instructing you on how to have successful experiences on the astral plane, giving you a better idea of what you might expect during your practice.

This chapter provides tips for recognizing when you're ready for separation from your physical body and understanding the sensations you may encounter during the first separation attempts. It also offers several techniques for making your first projection attempts, grounding for a safe start and return, and navigating the beginning of your journey in the astral state.

How Does Separation Feel?

Practitioners can experience a broad range of phenomena at the initial separation. For example, some may notice an intense tingling all over their body. This can vary from a pins and needles sensation to what almost feels like a mild electric shock. It's not painful, but it may be somewhat uncomfortable if you aren't used to it. It's normal, and once you choose to embrace it, it won't bother you anymore.

You need to focus on really tapping into what separation feels like."

Some practitioners can also hear sounds or see visions, even with their eyes closed. Some pick up on the sensation of being a separate entity from their physical body. Others only notice that they feel odd – as if something is different about their body. Some feel intense vibrations from the get-go, while others simply feel weightless without any other sensation.

You may also feel like you're floating away from your body. Some describe it as the feeling of drifting toward the sky and hovering up there as if they were a balloon or a bird. Perhaps this is one of the most peaceful and liberating sensations you can experience during this event. Giving you a sense of peace can dissipate your fears and boost your confidence in your ability to safely get through the experience.

If you pick up on vibrations or tingling, you may feel like these sensations are urging you to leave your body. The more you focus on separating yourself, the more they encourage you. They become stronger and stronger. They can be overwhelming – but don't worry. They aren't harmful. Remain calm and let them guide you. Breathe deeply in and out through your nose to relax your body and mind even more. The more you relax, the easier the separation becomes.

Giving in to the urge to leave your body may feel unnatural. This is normal, too. You may feel like you need to return. Focus on moving forward. Let it happen. It may not happen the first time. This is okay. You may need to practice before letting go and simply embracing the initial sensations. You may need time to understand they're there to guide you through the process. Give yourself the time and space you need until you feel safe enough to embrace these feelings and start the separation.

The Vibrational State

You might wonder how you will know when you're ready to separate from your physical body. You'll know you're ready when you reach the vibrational state. What does this state feel like? It can be a buzzing sensation traveling through your body. Or, you may feel a constant humming coming from inside your body and spreading throughout it. These sensations are caused by strong energy vibrations across your body.

You can only achieve this vibrational state if you're attempting to project in a comfortable space where you can focus without distractions and unwind.

When you start feeling the vibrations, try to settle even more. The more profound your relaxation becomes, the easier it will be for you to pick up the high-frequency vibrations and separate yourself from your physical body.

If focusing on the vibrations doesn't do the trick, try combining them with a vision of a radiant light. As you see this light descending on you and filling you with positivity, you will be able to embrace the vibrations that come with it, enveloping you with powerful energy.

After reaching the vibrational state, you'll notice that the vibrations will become more pronounced. You'll feel them in every tissue and particle of your body from head to toe. You will feel them in your subtle body, too. Immerse yourself in the experience and allow yourself to feel the sensations that carry you away from your physical body.

Achieving the vibrational state and working with it to help you separate yourself from your physical body takes patience and practice. By practicing diligently, you can harness the benefits of this state and the realm it carries you to.

Common Concerns and Fears During the First Projection Attempts

You're about to embark on a new and exciting experience, but you don't exactly know what to expect. This can cause fear and anxiety, which is entirely normal. You might worry you won't be able to return safely to your physical body because you haven't tried it before. Or, you may fear you'll get stuck during separation and won't even be able to attempt projection. Trying something you haven't done before can be intimidating, but it doesn't have to be. Astral projection is a natural process. Your soul knows what to do. You just have to help it remember and practice until it does.

If you've attempted projection before and felt uneasy and disoriented, you may hesitate to try it again. That is normal, too. However, having one or two bad experiences doesn't mean all your attempts will go the same way.

Try relaxation techniques before your first projection attempts to dissipate your fears and reassure yourself. Visualization, meditation, and deep breathing can relax your body and mind, making it easier to leave your worries behind and focus on the task.

Positive affirmations can also help you let go of your fears and concerns. By repeating positive statements, you remind yourself that you're in control. Nothing will happen without your consent. You set the intention to do something, and this is what you will do.

By letting go of fears, you're opening up to immensely enlightening experiences. Don't let your worries prevent you from doing this. Put an end to them before any astral projection attempts.

The Importance of Focus and Intention

One of the biggest mistakes beginners make is not putting enough effort toward focusing and setting intentions before the beginning of their journey. As a result, instead of having a controlled and productive journey, they end up wandering aimlessly in the astral realm. In some cases, the lack of focus can even cause an individual to struggle to separate their astral body from the physical one.

Meditation can help enhance focus and create awareness of everything you want to concentrate on. It encourages you to quiet your mind and relax your body so you can enter into a state where you can have an out-of-body experience and start astral travel. Regular meditation can improve your ability to focus on the different sensations, as well as your intention of having a safe astral journey.

A distraction-free environment is also crucial to maintaining focus. By eliminating distractions, you can concentrate on navigating through the steps of separation, journeying, and return. Anything that may disturb you can cause you to pause mid-separation or return abruptly to your body. This may further add to your fears of whether you'll be able to project safely.

Setting intention is crucial, and so is focusing on it. As a beginner, you want to learn how to set an intention for various parts of the process, from preparation to return. Each intention you set will reinforce the idea that you know what you're doing, making you more confident in your ability to journey safely.

The Role of Sight and Perception in the Astral Plane

As your senses aren't used to exploring what's beyond the physical world, your first experiences may not be the best. When you try to visualize something during your astral journey, it may appear blurry or incomplete. This is because your projection isn't stable yet. Once it does, everything will be clear from the get-go.

There are ways you can practice improving your sight and perception. Preparatory meditation exercises are a wonderful way to start. They foster a deep focus and awareness of the senses and what you can pick up with them. Here, it's crucial to remember that your intuition is a sense you will rely on, so you must also practice sharpening it.

How do you hone your intuition? The best way to do it is to spend more time attempting astral projection and connecting to the astral state. The more attempts you make, the more attuned you become to what works and what doesn't. Your intuition will tell you how, and you will learn to rely on it.

You can improve your perception in the astral state by learning to differentiate between your physical and astral body. You can do this during your first separation attempts by noticing how each feels. The sensation will hit them differently, so learning how each feels is a wonderful way to improve your perception in the astral plane. During your attempts, you'll only need to focus on the sensations in your astral body.

Grounding Exercise for Safe Return

Many beginners feel uneasy about returning. Some fear they won't be able to return safely or they will lose their balance. A quick grounding exercise helps you feel connected to the physical world. This adds to your feeling of safety and ensures a smooth return, dissipating your worries about possible trouble you may encounter when you return. You only have to focus on the sensations in your physical body and the connection with nature. Nature is a powerful grounding tool as it promotes the sense of being present and draws away negativity from the practitioner.

Instructions:
1. You can choose to lie down during the astral projection part. However, in this preparatory exercise, sitting or standing is best. Keeping your feet on the ground makes it easier to create a connection to nature and center yourself. You can always lie down later before you begin your astral journey.
2. Take a few deep breaths and feel yourself relaxing.
3. Imagine small roots appearing at your feet, sprouting from them, and descending into the earth. See them grow and become larger until they look like the roots of a massive tree.
4. Focus on the connection between the earth and the vines growing from your feet. Feel yourself anchored in place. Engrave the memory of the connection and its feeling into your mind. This will be your anchor wherever you travel.
5. As you become more and more grounded, you'll feel a steady flow of energy coursing through your connection with the earth. Positive energy comes up, and negative energy goes down. It's leaving you, so you can only focus on the positive feelings in your body and let this bring you back.
6. Continue with the exercise until you feel bored and the fear of not being able to return has dissipated.

The Rope Technique

This technique is one of the most recommended ways for beginners to experience astral projection. It's easy enough to master, yet it's effective and ensures you can have a safe trip. For the safest journeys, do this when you're fully rested to avoid falling asleep. The morning after a good night's sleep is the best time to try this.

Imagine reaching for a rope and working your way up.[13]

Instructions:

1. Close your eyes and relax to clear your mind and improve your focus. You want to be able to focus as much as possible, as this will help you return safely to your physical body. Notice the sensations in your body, starting at your toes and all the way up to the top of your head.
2. Take deep breaths until your body and mind are relaxed. As you relax, reassure yourself you're in complete control. This will help you loosen up even more.
3. Once you've reached a state of profound relaxation, switch your attention from your breathing and sensations in your physical body to creating a vision. If you have trouble visualizing, try tuning into the vibrations around you. You will be able to control these vibrations as you connect to them. Then, you'll be able to control your mind's ability to visualize, as well.
4. Imagine looking up and seeing a rope tied above you. See yourself reach for it with your hands. Touch it. How does it feel? How does the texture feel on your hands? This will help reinforce the vision and connect with it.
5. Grab the rope with both hands and see yourself pulling yourself up on it. Put one hand over the other, pull the second hand over the first one, and so on.
6. Climbing the rope can trigger the separation process, so be prepared. At one point, you'll feel yourself moving up on the road and away from your physical body, too. You may also experience the first signs of separation, like floating, vibration, or slight dizziness and confusion, so don't let them distract you. Continue focusing on pulling yourself up and away from your physical self and into the astral plane.
7. When you start feeling the deep vibrations, focus on them. You're almost there. Imagine the vibrations permeating every inch of your body. Slowly, by focusing solely on the vibrations, you'll find yourself away from your body and in the astral plane.

The Roll-Out Method

The rolling-out method is a great way to practice separation from the physical body. You gradually shift your focus from your physical body to your astral body until you can only focus on the latter. Once you only feel it moving, you prepare to shift perspective and roll out of your physical self and into the astral plane.

Instructions:
1. Find a quiet and comfortable space.
2. Lie on your back and close your eyes.
3. Focus on relaxing your body and mind. Breathe deeply in and out through your nose.
4. Once you feel relaxed, shift your attention to the sensations in your body. How do you feel? Do you feel comfortable? Do you feel the weight of your body? How does it feel lying down?
5. Continue tuning in and analyzing the sensations in your physical body. Feel yourself relaxing even more.
6. Now, visualize yourself inside your body. Not how you see your body in the mirror but an image of your subtle body lying within your physical one.
7. Set your intentions for astral travel. Start with the intention of separating your astral body from the physical one.
8. Tell yourself you're ready to roll out of your physical body.
9. At this point, you may feel yourself reaching the vibrational state or floating sensation, both of which signal you're ready to begin your journey.
10. Imagine your astral body rolling left to right or back and forth within your physical body. It's moving slowly at first, then gaining momentum until you feel like you want to lift up and out of your body. Your physical body remains still. Only your astral body is moving.
11. Keep rolling back and forth and focus on the movement. Don't focus on your physical body. Keep rolling until the movement becomes natural. Do it until you shift perspectives and feel you're about to roll out of your body and enter the astral plane.

12. When you feel ready, roll out and start your astral projection experience until you're fully separated from your body. Then, prepare to observe, imagine, and explore whatever you wish.
13. It may take practice until you can roll it out successfully. Separation isn't always easy. Be patient and consistent. Remain calm, embrace the sensations, and let them guide you through the natural process of leaving your physical body.

The Floating Technique

The floating balloon technique is one of the safest options for astral travel. It guides you toward embracing the natural sensation of floating you'll experience after separation. It also gives you control over the process. You can choose where you want to go. All you need to do is follow the balloon and let it help you relax.

Instructions:
1. Find a comfortable place where you won't be disturbed. Wear loose-fitting clothes and take off any jewelry that may make you uncomfortable or distract you as you try to relax.
2. Lie on a mat or bed.
3. Let your eyes close slowly, naturally.
4. Draw a deep breath, filling your lungs. Then, let it out. Continue breathing deeply until your body adapts to a natural flow of deep breathing.
5. Notice how your body begins to relax. Allow this sensation to travel through your body.
6. Focus on your breathing until you feel completely loose and limber. All the muscles relax, there is no tension in your body, and your mind is calm.
7. You feel completely relaxed, light, and comfortable.
8. Imagine seeing a beautiful blue sky above your head. You notice a large balloon floating in the sky as you admire it.
9. See it glide toward you. It's glowing with a golden light. It makes you feel warm and even more relaxed.
10. Visualize yourself becoming lighter and lighter.
11. As you see the balloon nearing you, you feel so light, as if you can lift slowly off the ground. Feel free to give in to this sensation.

Feel yourself following the balloon up toward the sky. Immerse yourself in the liberating feeling of floating.

12. Continue focusing on the floating sensation. It may be an unusual sensation at first, but let it envelop you. Remain calm. You feel safe and relaxed.
13. When you feel completely safe and peaceful, look down. Notice how high you've traveled from your body. See how far you've followed the balloon.

Stabilizing Astral Vision

You can start exploring your surroundings once you feel you've been successfully separated from your body. At first, you may experience some blurriness when looking around. Or, you may be able to glance at something but don't know what it is. It's like the information is at the back of your mind, but you can't make out what it is. This is completely normal. With practice, your vision during astral travel will become sharper, and you'll be able to focus more on deciphering what you see. The more time you spend in the astral plane, the easier it will be.

Do you know what else can help besides regular practice? A little affirmation exercise right after separation.

Instructions:

1. As you transition to the astral state, imagine you're rubbing your hands together. Do this for a few moments, then wait to see whether your vision stabilizes. If it does and you gain awareness of your surroundings, you can continue your journey.
2. If your vision hasn't stabilized, put your hands together and say, *"I need clarity now."* Wait again to check if you can see it clearly. If you can, continue your journey.

Returning to the Physical Body

Grounding yourself after returning from astral travel is just as crucial as doing it before your journey. Without it, your return may be a little bumpy; you may become dizzy once you reunite with your body and feel fatigued or spacey for hours afterward. You may also be confused or feel like you've lost track of big chunks of time. Fortunately, you can prevent this and return safely by grounding yourself with the following exercise. The goal is to let your subtle body slowly align with your physical body.

Make sure to do it after every astral attempt, even if you haven't traveled far. It will make you feel safer and more confident in your ability to practice astral projection.

Instructions:
1. When you feel ready to return, set the intention.
2. Then, start breathing deeply. Imagine you're slowly returning to your physical body. You can feel your soul sinking back into its physical receptacle.
3. Continue breathing deeply as you transition from feeling weightlessness to feeling the weight of your limbs. Do you notice any sensations in them? What about underneath you? How does the surface you lie on feel?
4. Focus on feeling your connection to the surface underneath you. If you're on the floor, touch the ground with your palms.
5. Take your time to adjust to the new sensations. The reconnection between your body and soul will be automatic. Nevertheless, it may take a few minutes, especially if you've just started practicing projection.
6. Open your eyes and slowly notice everything around you. You've returned from your trip. When you feel ready, you can continue with your daily activities. If you need more time, you can replenish your energy by drinking a glass of water, eating a small snack, or holding a crystal for a few minutes.

Chapter 5: Exploring Dimensions Beyond the Earthly Matrix

One of the reasons many seek to master the art of astral projection is to be able to roam around the vast dimensions beyond the physical plane. As you'll learn from this chapter, scouring these fascinating landscapes has many advantages. This chapter offers guidance for exploring the higher planes, understanding their significance, distinguishing between them, and navigating them with confidence and clarity.

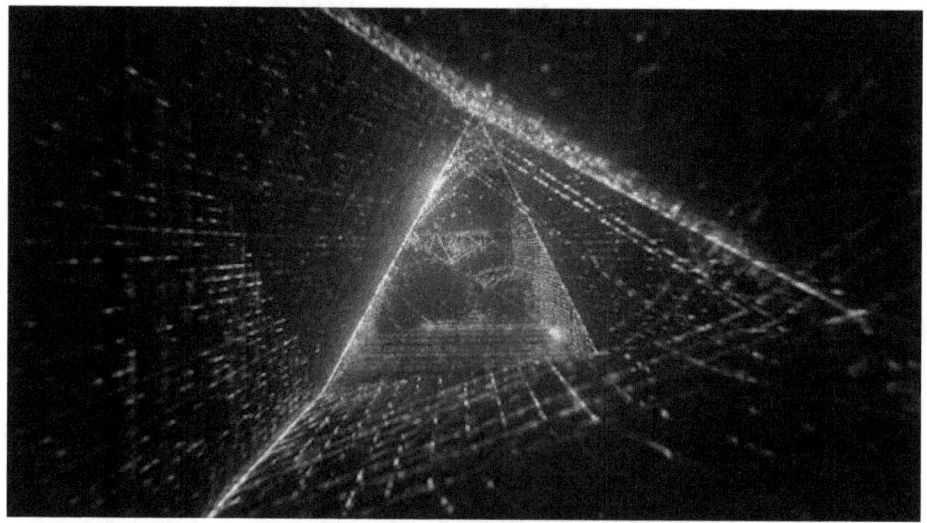

You can explore different dimensions through out-of-body experiences.[18]

The Higher Dimensions

Higher dimensions are layers of existence above the physical plane. The physical plane is where you live (what your physical body inhabits) and experience it with your physical senses. Just as this plane has unique characteristics, frequencies, and inhabitants, so does every other plane.

The Astral Plane

The next plane after the physical one is the astral plane. This is usually the first place newcomers visit for astral projection. This place is linked to desires and emotions. If you've just started practicing astral projection, you're still tied to the desires of the physical plane. When you start projecting, you'll end up at a place that is still familiar: the astral plane. This is natural. Departed souls often linger in the astral realm before moving up to higher planes.

The Mental Plane

Next is the mental plane, the realm where you can analyze your thoughts and ideas more profoundly. Associated with thinking and the power of the mind, the mental plane is a good place for learning new skills. You may encounter others looking for intellectual growth.

The Causal Plane

The next plane is associated with intention and manifestation. This is the causal plane. It is where you can empower your intention in spiritual work and manifest your wants and needs. If you want to connect with your higher self, the causal plane is the place to be. Here, you can find spiritual wisdom, enlightenment, and purpose.

The Spiritual Plane

Those ready to step up to an even higher level of spiritual existence can explore the spiritual plane. Here, you can connect with divine powers and celestial beings, revering in oneness with these purely enlightened entities. Only consciousness exists on the spiritual plane, and all remnants of the physical world are left behind.

Even if you don't have a specific goal for exploring one of these planes, visiting them presents many benefits. They can teach you more about your spiritual being, help you grow spiritually, and realize your purpose in life. For some, visiting the higher dimensions is the first step toward recognizing their innate spirituality and need for enlightenment.

By collecting wisdom from the higher dimensions, you have the potential to become the best version of yourself. You learn that everything is possible. You only need to want it strongly enough.

Besides deepening the connection with yourself, higher spiritual beings, and the universe, visiting the higher dimensions can increase your sense of peace and well-being. It's like tapping into an oasis of tranquility because you know how much you'll benefit from your journeys.

Exploring the higher dimension allows you to expand your consciousness. Stepping onto the astral realm is already a wonderful way to enrich your consciousness. Continuing toward the other planes will provide you with even greater perspectives. As you recognize the interconnectedness of everything, you start living a more purposeful and meaningful life. You'll discover that while you have a purpose as an individual entity, your contribution to the universe has a much higher purpose.

The planes of the higher dimensions often align with different energy frequencies, which is most noticeable during transitions. Your perception changes when you go from one realm to another because you pick up different vibrational frequencies. Once you make several visits to the diverse realms, you'll be able to pick up and adjust to the new frequencies right away.

Transitioning to Higher Dimensions

Each plane has a unique purpose, and depending on how attuned you are to their purposes, the transition between them may happen automatically. The realms are interconnected, and their energies can influence each other. However, you may not realize this right away.

There are several ways you can recognize a transition. One is to pay attention to patterns. For example, only the mental and astral planes have patterns associated with emotions and thoughts. You may also notice that your perception of time changes. The higher you go, the less perception you'll have of time. At first, you'll see that time goes faster or slower than before. However, the higher you go, the less you'll notice how fast time passes.

Your intuition will work differently, too. The more your connectedness to your spirituality is elevated, the more you'll be drawn to your gut feelings. A sure sign of transitioning to a different dimension is that you want to explore what your intuition tells you about your perception of your surroundings. You may notice you can pick up on danger or others' intentions in certain dimensions when you weren't able to do this in the previous dimension you visited.

Tuning in to new visual or sensory cues is another way to recognize transitions between dimensions. You may have more vivid mental imagery than you had before. Or, your visions may become more frequent or specific. Your perception of energy shifts can change, too. You couldn't pick up on energetic influences, and now you suddenly can? It may be because you have hopped onto another plane. Some even experience changes in their own vibrations. You're getting attuned to the vibrational frequency of your surroundings, so it makes sense your energy changes, too.

Enhanced awareness is another trademark of a dimensional shift. You may find yourself more connected to your surroundings or the universe. You suddenly notice colors, textures, vibrancy, smells, and noises in a new dimension. If you do, this is likely because you have shifted to a new dimension where you can (and likely should) experience this heightened awareness.

An amplified or changed intuition isn't a coincidence. Experiences you encounter, including vivid or symbolic imagery, different beings, and landscapes, can vary. Interpreting them is also a personal process. You can learn to interpret them by honing your intuition. You should also start practicing and being open to new experiences. Recording your experiences in a journal can also help. As you revisit them, you may find connections or answers to questions you had overlooked, and you can finally interpret the wisdom you've gathered.

Some experiences may be unusual, but you'll only see what you are meant to see. When you're ready, you'll always return to your physical body safely, regardless of which dimension you're visiting. Your body remains in the physical realm, so you'll always be drawn back to it.

Exploring the Astral Plane

Once you've successfully separated from your physical body, remain near your immediate surroundings to familiarize yourself with the astral plane. From here, you can start exploring details of your environment, noting any differences from the physical world.

Try to familiarize yourself with the astral plane.[14]

Examine the objects you see around you. Is there something you have seen in the physical world but haven't paid much attention to how it looks? If yes, start by taking a close look at it. What color is it? How big is it? What shape is it? Gather as many details as possible about the object.

Next, you can walk around the space and see what else you notice. Are there any patterns, colors, objects, or anything else that stands out? Take your time exploring. How different is what you see from your experiences on the physical plane? What makes it different? What do you perceive differently?

It's a good idea to only visit familiar places during your first projection attempts. You can explore them in depth and create points you can return to when you feel uncertain or unsafe during your explorations. You can go a little farther each time, but only as far as you're comfortable. Also, going too far may be overwhelming if there are too many things to explore and take in from your environment.

Navigating Symbolic Landscapes

During your travel, you may come across vivid landscapes or symbolic imagery you may not recognize. Feel free to explore them. You're likely meant to see them for a reason.

Have an open mind and be curious during your travels. Just because something you see doesn't make sense right away, it doesn't mean it doesn't have a meaning to your life or spiritual journey. So, if you see something you don't recognize, stop and give yourself time to ponder on it. Ask yourself why you are seeing it. What reason could there be to see it? Could it be connected to any part of your life? What relation would your experience have to where you are in your spiritual journey?

Connecting to the Energy Grid

The astral grid is the network of energy that connects all dimensions and everyone and everything in them. This grid is crucial in making your travels across the planes possible. The different lines in the network influence each other and can be influenced by entities and even your energy. Knowing you can affect the grid and take you wherever you want to go are good facts to know – they make it easier to connect to the universal energy network and explore the higher dimensions.

Instructions:
1. Start with your usual preparatory exercises and relaxation techniques.
2. Once you're completely relaxed, set your intention to become wholeheartedly open to new experiences. You want to be receptive to connecting with all the positive energies you're meant to encounter on your journeys. Setting the intention to be open to tap into these energies is crucial for forging a connection with the grid.
3. Continue focusing on your intention until you feel confident in your openness to new frequencies.
4. Next, switch your focus to your subtle body and away from your physical self. Do this until you complete your separation.
5. Focus on the vibrations you can pick up with your energy body. Set the intention of wanting to connect and harness the energy around you. See it as something empowering (because it is) and supportive of your journey. Don't be afraid of it.

6. Receiving the energy from the grid may feel unusual at first. Yet, if you intend to harness it, you won't receive more than you need. You won't be exposed to anything you didn't give permission for.
7. Once you embrace the vibrations around you and connect to the grid, reflect on what it can give you. Perhaps it can provide security on your travels. Maybe it can help you understand how astral travel works and what you must do to make your projections successful.
8. Continue maintaining your connection until it feels comfortable. This may only be for a few minutes. That's okay. Go at your own pace. When you feel ready to return, set the intention, and you'll float right back into your physical body.

Connecting with Angels and Light Beings

Angels and light beings are wonderful helpers in any spiritual exploration. By building a connection with them, you can receive many blessings, including guidance when you feel stuck or encounter difficulties.

Instructions:
1. Start the separation process in your preferred way.
2. When you've reached the astral state, visualize a beam of white light appearing over you. Then, the light starts projecting down, washing over you.
3. Feel your energy being cleansed and your vibrations attuned to higher frequencies. Feel yourself becoming confident in being able to connect with any angel or light being you'll encounter.
4. Do a quick check of how you feel. What emotions are you feeling now? Do you feel excited? Are you curious? Having an open mind is fundamental for successful communication with celestial beings. Is there anything in particular you want to learn from the entity?
5. Now, set the intention to invoke the angel or light being you want to talk to. You may already have done a little research and know who may be the most helpful. If you didn't, simply state what you need help with. The right being will find you.

6. Wait until they hear your call. You can explore a little. You may even feel the need to move forward or go to a certain place. This is your intuition telling you where you'll find the assistance you're looking for.
7. Suddenly, you notice an orb of light appearing in the distance, like the one in the beginning, just much brighter. It comes closer and closer to you. You may be able to distinguish its form. You may continue to see only a shape enveloped in light.
8. When it reaches you, you will feel the being's energy pulsating. As it connects to your energy, you feel warm, protected, and reassured.
9. You can ask the being any question you want. Wait for their answer. It may not come in the form you expect it to. It may come in a vision, a symbolic message, etc. Trust your intuition to be able to receive and decipher it.
10. When you've got all the answers you need, offer gratitude to the angel/light being. Release them and promise you'll contact them again. They will appreciate it if you show you want to build a connection with them. In your next travels, they might appear spontaneously and guide you where you need to go.

Soaring Through the Cosmos

Are you looking for inspiration to decide where to go or what to explore? If so, this exercise will help you find it by soaring through the cosmos and discovering wonderful sights.

Explore the vast world of the cosmos.[15]

Instructions:
1. Start your transition in your preferred way.
2. As you separate from your physical body, imagine seeing nothing but darkness around you.
3. Suddenly, you're lifted into the darkness, floating up into the emptiness. You're going up higher and higher and faster and faster.
4. Then, you notice flickering lights appear around you. They're swirling around, their colors indistinguishable at first and then turning into a vortex of vivid colors.
5. At last, you emerge from this color vortex. You look around and see you're in the cosmos. You see stars, planets, and nebulae around you.
6. Fly past each object and enjoy the powerful feeling of being able to experience the cosmos up close. You're in control. You can go wherever you want to.
7. Continue soaring among the planets and celestial objects until you feel you've seen enough. Then, set the intention to come back, and soon, you'll be reunited with your physical body.

Visiting Your Sacred Library (Akasha)

In the higher dimensions, there is a place where the records of thoughts, emotions, actions, and experiences of every soul are kept. This vast library of knowledge is called the *Akasha* or *Akashic Records* and can be accessed through astral projection. This is a truly empowering journey, but it can be demanding as it requires you to focus on what you're doing the entire time. For the same reason, make sure to set your intention of visiting your sacred library before you start projecting.

Instructions:
1. Start astral projection via your preferred method.
2. Once you've separated, bring your intention into focus. You'll move toward the place where your records are kept. Your intuition may show you a picture of what this place looks like, making it easier to find your way there.
3. If this is your first time visiting your Akasha, you may wish to call on a spiritual guide to help you through the process. A guide may appear on their own as soon as you get near your records. You

can ask them any questions about your records. For example, you can ask them about specific experiences.
4. Your guide will show you the answer in some form. For example, the answers may appear like pictures on a movie screen in front of your eyes. This may be a very emotionally charged experience, so try to remain in control of your feelings. Otherwise, you may be propelled back into your body.
5. Your guide will show you everything you need to know about the experience you inquired about. However, after the first few times, you may feel like you have more questions than answers. This is normal. Over time, you'll learn how to interpret what you've discovered, leaving you with more answers with every visit.
6. Record your experience and whatever you've discovered in a journal. You'll be able to revisit them later with a different perspective, and you may find answers to some of the questions you feel were left unanswered during your visit.
7. If you wish, you can build a little nook for yourself in or near your library. You can start doing this during your first visit. Just create an image of your perfect, cozy reading spot. Be as detailed as possible, and keep this image in your focus for a few minutes. Next time you visit your records, your little nook will be waiting for you, welcoming you to explore whatever you want to learn from your records.

Meeting Extraterrestrials and Higher-Dimensional Beings

During your travels, you can meet fellow spiritual seekers from the physical world, other planes, or even other universes. These extraterrestrial beings may offer even more guidance and wisdom as they may be more advanced spiritually. Likewise, you can also come across other beings living in higher dimensions, like ascended masters or archangels. Ascended masters are spiritual seekers who reached the highest state of spiritual enlightenment and now guide others on their spiritual journeys. If you want to learn from these entities, you can connect to them while projecting. They'll be more than happy to help.

Instructions:

1. Find a comfortable place. Sit with your feet firmly on the ground. Whenever you're ready, close your eyes.
2. Take a deep breath and hold it. As you do, feel the energy rising up your spine. Release the breath, then repeat.
3. Allow your breath to fall back into a natural rhythm. Starting at the top of your head, search your body for tension, and release any you find until you feel everything inside you relax.
4. Imagine you're sitting on the top of a hill on a dark, cool night. See small roots sprouting from your body, digging and carving through the ground beneath you. Through these roots, feel the energy from the ground enveloping you, starting from your legs and going all the way up to your highest chakras.
5. See the energy become a beam of light as it leaves your head and travels toward the sky. Follow the beam of light to the sky and across the universe with your subtle body. Set the intention of wanting to follow the light and see yourself moving upwards.
6. Suddenly, you notice that your presence has been noted. You feel entities reacting to you, beckoning you to follow them across the universe. You see a brilliant white beam approaching you. You can feel its warmth as if you're connected to their energy.
7. Open yourself to the connection with this being. Allow them to reach out to you and communicate what they want you to learn. Receive your energy in your heart. You may not be able to see their true form (higher beings rarely have a particular form), but you'll be able to receive their support.
8. Maintain your connection with the higher being as long as you wish. They may leave you earlier. If they do, it's because they've provided the help you needed at the time. You may encounter them on another trip. Once you practice more, you'll be able to call on specific entities and ask them for guidance.

Exploring Celestial/Cosmic Gardens, Cities, and Other Universes

What if you want to explore alone? Perhaps you don't need guidance or don't want to connect with anyone but want to do some astral sightseeing instead. During astral projection, you can visit universes, cities, celestial gardens, or any other place you wish. You can get inspiration by finding a picture of how you would imagine the destination would look. You can even leave it all to your intuition and creativity and let the journey take you places.

Instructions:
1. Sit comfortably with your hands on the top of your thighs and your feet planted firmly on the ground.
2. Take a deep breath through your nose, and let it out. Take another deep breath and hold it. Before letting go, release the tension from your body. Continue until you feel relaxed.
3. Visualize the location you want to go. If you don't have a specific destination in mind, state that you want to visit another universe, celestial city, etc. If you know where you want to go, state it into your intention and bring an image of it into your mind.
4. Then, become aware of the surface you're sitting on. Imagine yourself sinking into the chair. Allow the relaxation to go all the way to every part of your body.
5. Imagine you're looking out a window, admiring the sunset. As the sun sets, you notice the darkness settling. Then, the first stars come out.
6. The more stars you see, the closer you feel yourself to them and farther from your body until you feel yourself drifting completely away from your body.
7. As you float upwards and above the trees, you feel safe and confident. Soon, you find yourself among the clouds. Then, you pass them until you arrive among the stars.
8. Notice the unique sound you hear. Can you pick up the direction it's coming from? Travel in that direction. It will take you to your first destination.

9. Once you arrive at your first destination, feel free to explore it. What do you see there? For example, if you're visiting a city, you may be able to admire its stunning and unique buildings and layout. If you're visiting a garden, you may gaze at all the wonderful colors and natural beauties you find there.
10. Continue soaring until you wish, then set your intention to return.

Chapter 6: Overcoming Fear and Barriers to Astral Travel

There's an enchantment and allure about journeying beyond the Matrix and reaching new spiritual horizons. Still, you'd be hard-pressed to find a beginner who fearlessly jumps into this adventure head-on. It's normal to feel some trepidation about separating from your body and what you perceive to be objective reality.

Overcome your fear of losing control.[16]

Fears of losing control of the experience, an inability to return to your physical body, and the concept of making the unconscious conscious are ubiquitous among beginners. However, these fish-out-of-water jitters will subside. Many experienced astral travelers often describe how their initial fears transformed into moments of courage, self-discovery, and self-empowerment, enabling them to deepen their practice and trust the process.

This chapter will help you do the same by exploring emotional and psychological barriers that may arise during your OBE, reframing your jitters, and understanding that they are an opportunity for growth. With the practical strategies laid out in this chapter, you can overcome these fears and cultivate resilience. You will reach a sense of calm and confidence as you navigate challenges and break through any barriers holding you back from astral travel.

The Root of Common Fears Associated with Astral Travel

Fearing what you have never experienced is natural, and so is feeling apprehensive about OBEs. These fears stem from your mind's default instincts, which exist to keep you grounded and safe in unfamiliar situations.

The root of common fears are:
1. Fear of the unknown
2. Loss of control
3. Encountering negative entities and unsettling imagery

Fear of the Unknown

This is the most common fear. You might wonder what it will feel like to leave your body, what you will see, and how you will be sure you can return. It's difficult to imagine these things the same way it is hard to imagine a road you've never traveled on. To mentally itself, your mind might be incessantly trying to map it out by wondering what dangers may lurk ahead.

The truth is that none of your thoughts can define what you have yet to encounter. You can't simply think your way into *doing*; you actually have to do it. You have to make a conscious effort to trust yourself. Think of moments where you're lost in your imagination. You allow it to carry you away without fear of how you'll return. Or, consider when you lay your head down to sleep at night, hoping to be enraptured by a sweet dream. You don't lie awake at night worrying that your dream might become a nightmare. You just trust your subconscious.

You have always experienced dreams. You probably don't even give them a second thought – but now, imagine describing daydreaming to someone who's never been through it. They would feel the same unfamiliarity you feel about astral projection. Dreaming sounds eerie and terrifying. However, you know that their fears of the unknown can be tempered through realization and actualization.

Loss of Control

The fear of losing control stems from the idea that you're losing touch with reality. It's the spontaneity of it all that makes you think you won't be able to steer the adventure in the way you'd like.

Luckily, astral projection does not require you to let go as you venture out of the ordinary. Instead, it helps you focus on what you can control to make yourself comfortable. Know what you're doing and what you hope to accomplish. Keep this phrase in mind: "What you expect to see is what you're likely to see." If you focus on what you cannot control, you might make that fear a certainty.

The good news is this means you're simply focusing on the wrong thing. Just as lucid dreaming gives a person a chance to paint their own dreamy canvas, astral projection allows you to decide what the intention of your trip is.

Bring back your childlike spirit of adventure. Children are often ludic and fearless when they go into their imaginations. The idea of floating or flying doesn't scare them. They don't allow fear to turn these sensations into one of drowning or falling. Viewing astral projection in a similar light will help you rationalize and overcome your fear of losing control.

Bear in mind that you go where your thoughts go, and your thoughts are merely musings, not reality – unless you want them to be. Trust your potential, meditate with intention, and you'll see it's up to you to lead your thoughts; don't let them lead you. Once you understand that you can control yourself, you won't be burdened by the need to control external factors.

Encountering Negative Entities or Unsettling Imagery

It's hard not to get wrapped up in contemplations and scrutiny when considering an OBE. When stepping into uncharted territory, you'll wonder who you'll meet, if they'll disturb you, or if you'll disturb them. Will your experience with spiritual entities be smooth and unhurried or sudden and unforgiving?

The fear of encountering negative entities and unsettling imagery can be an ominous presence hanging over your head like a dark cloud. However, the truth is that it is all in your head. Remember, this fear is a result of feeling not in control. You have all the tools to protect yourself from harm, and one of them is your energy. Since this fear is typically due to not knowing how to manage your astral travel, devising an exit and re-entry plan will help your body relax and ease into the process.

You can work on becoming open and intent on experiencing positivity and light. This not only helps you avoid these unsettling experiences but it also helps you redirect your focus if they appear. To gain the confidence that you can and will be in control of your journey, remember these three keys: visualization, intention, and guidance. Visualize a protective shield of light, set clear intentions, and call on your spirit guides to safely lead you through your journey.

Think of the three S's: Sight, Sound, and Scent. Whenever unwanted thoughts creep in, redirect your attention to what you can see, hear, and smell. You'll then be able to bring your mind to where you want to go during an unwanted encounter. You'll know to focus on your goals instead of your fears and how to visualize your protection in the form of a light shield so you're in the proper frame of mind to call upon your spirit guides.

It's best to practice setting these intentions and visualizations before attempting astral projection. Be in tune with your senses when negative thoughts or feelings come up. This will help you develop the state of mind you must be in when encountering negative entities in the world beyond. Focus is conscious awareness and a powerful tool in directing your rising thoughts toward positive results whenever they bubble up.

Fears have only as much power as you grant them. They become real when you allow them to. While your subconscious has quite the imagination, it is not leading the charge here; your unconscious self is. You are making the unconscious conscious. This means you can erase your fears as quickly as you created them. By understanding your goals and rehearsing the rituals you will learn throughout this chapter, you will move with conscious awareness and intention, not fear and interruptions.

What Could Be Blocking Your Astral Journey?

Common emotional and psychological barriers, such as fears, disillusionment, and self-doubt, can be broken through small, daily habits. How you manage daily activities impacts your ability to raise your vibration when trying to achieve an OBE. A few things in the physical world that could be blocking you from entering the astral world are:

Home and Environment – Organizing your home is a gateway to organizing your thoughts. If your environment creates a sense of insecurity and a lack of trust and structure, it will be hard to achieve the opposite on an astral journey.

Diet and Exercise – Sedentary lifestyles and unhealthy foods don't fuel your energy; they take away from it. This impacts your quality of sleep and rest.

Living in Fear – Consider your approach to dealing with uncertainties in the physical world. How you manage these will provide insight into what you need to work on. Do you cower in fear and become paralyzed by self-doubt when attempting something new? If so, it's time to change your frequency. Take that nervous energy and learn to breathe through it, release it, and replace it with calmness.

Is Astral Projection Safe?

Many beginners conclude that astral projection isn't safe before doing any research, mainly because it is often conflated with the OBEs that occur with near-death experiences. People's bad memories of the latter instill fear, preventing them from ever attempting to revisit the notion of leaving their physical bodies. The clear difference between the two motifs is that astral projection is an *intentional* OBE.

Remember that experiences like these are subjective, and many trials are done with minimal research and understanding. You can be like the many others who harmlessly traversed through the astral plane by simply understanding that the journey can be controlled with practice.

You can rest assured that your astral travel is as safe as going to sleep every night and being enveloped in a dream. You don't fall asleep wondering if you'll wake up. You know you will, and you always wake up just fine. The same applies to the astral world. The connection between your astral and physical body is unbreakable.

Essentially, your astral body temporarily detaches from your physical body during sleep, knowing the bond can never be severed. This means that you engage in a form of astral projection every night when you nod off, and nothing has ever prevented your astral and physical bodies from reuniting after waking up. Learning about the scientific and spiritual aspects of the experience will reassure you of its safety. As you saw in Chapter 2, there is a neurological basis for astral travel.

With this in mind, you can conquer any fears of losing your sense of reality or safety, propelling you into the state of relaxation needed to reach out into the spiritual realm.

The Importance of Building Trust in the Process

The best way to dispel fear is through education. Read. Read. Read. The knowledge you gain will build your trust in the process. Dedicate thirty minutes a day to learning about astral projection, not just through books like these but also through others' testimonials and practicing the techniques you've studied. The more insight you gain, the more confident you'll be.

To develop your faith in it, you must demystify the entire process. This is where practice comes in. Below, you will learn to develop a sense of security through tested grounding techniques and positive affirmations.

How to Build Trust and a Sense of Security:
1. Visualize your astral body.
2. Ask for protection.
3. Ground yourself with exercises.
4. Use positive affirmations.

Visualize Your Astral Body

Visualization helps with concentration. As Star Wars' Qui Gon Jinn once said, "Your focus determines your reality." Practice visualizing the separation of your astral body from your physical one. An accessible method to enhance your focus and strengthen your visualization abilities is the rope technique, where you picture a rope hanging above your head, and your astral body uses it to climb beyond the physical world. This technique is also useful when exiting the realm.

Visualization Steps:

1. **Deep relaxation** – Relax your physical body by lying down and allowing yourself to fall into a half-asleep state.
2. **Create the desired mindset** – Focus on your mental energy instead of your physical one to create the heightened state needed to project.
3. **Picture lifting out of your body** – Focus on your muscles and cells and feel everything gradually elevating.
4. **Remain Aware** – Align with environmental vibrations as you ascend through the astral plane.

With each practice, you'll find accessing the astral world easier. Don't mentally exert yourself to get it right. It may take a few tries, so don't force the process. Set the tone with music, or find a comfortable position when you're ready to sleep. Little rituals like these help you remain consistent and visualize with intention. There is no need to put extreme expectations on yourself. You probably won't fully project on your first try. You might manage to separate consciousness from one body part at a time, helping you determine which body part needs to relax. With conscious efforts and dedicated practice, you will gradually increase the length of your practice and your ability to elevate your entire being.

Asking for Protection

Protection is received from spirit guides, supportive crystals, and your ancestors. As you raise your vibration levels, you'll be able to communicate with your spirit guides. Everybody has them. You just need to reach them by entering their dimension in the astral world – just as you would your ancestors. Your spirit guides and ancestors are your teachers, your wise guardians who advise you on the spiritual plane – and even protect and aid you in the physical world without you knowing.

Crystals help focus your energy. You need emotional control and consistency for astral projection. Crystals harness your energy, help you quieten distractions, and clear your mind of clouded thoughts, creating a more centered self. To practice harnessing your energy with crystals, use them in your daily routine and when you meditate.

You can also tailor your supportive tools to whatever makes you feel protected. Perhaps a specific scent or essential oil you use during a warm bath, a soothing jazz tune, or a protective symbol, such as a childhood blanket, is a better fit. Choose what helps you create the comforting atmosphere you need.

Grounding Exercises

Grounding exercises are practical strategies to overcome barriers in astral travel. Before engaging in these exercises, make sure you're in the right headspace. One way to get there is through the earthing mindset.

This mindset connects you with nature, thus helping you connect to your environment. Achieve this through:

- Walking on grass
- Gardening
- Swimming or lying in water

The goal is to come into your OBE in a calm, peaceful state. Then, you're prepared for your grounding strategies:

Deep Breathing - Focus on your breath to stay grounded and present. Inhale for four counts through your nose and exhale for four counts through your mouth. Feel your belly move up and down like waves ebbing and flowing to the shore.

Posture - Adopt a posture you can always return to. Consider lying down during meditation or getting in a position where your body feels relaxed so you can clearly envision grounding yourself.

The Five Senses - Visualize your surroundings. Look around for anything that activates your sense of taste, touch, hearing, smell, or sight. Focus on objects, touch them, and notice their details. The more senses you use, the more grounded you'll become.

Sleep - Let yourself sleep. Agitation or excitement is anxious energy that takes away your sense of control, which is the antithesis of grounding. A lack of rest is an obstacle to your practices and keeps you rigid and alert.

Keep rehearsing your strategies on the days or weeks leading up to your astral projection attempt.

Positive Affirmations

Positive affirmations reinforce your mental strength and reduce anxiety, reminding you that you're safe and in control.

- I am peaceful and relaxed.
- I am open-minded and conscious.
- I am protected and in control.
- I am resilient and capable.
- My mind and body are prepared for astral projection.
- I am certain I can achieve astral travel.
- I will be calm and aware.
- My astral and physical body are always aligned and connected.
- I will have a positive out-of-body experience.
- I will enjoy my OBE.
- I leave my physical body every night and return every morning.
- I can visualize astral projection and achieve it.
- Visualizations are becoming easier with each try.
- Astral travel will come naturally to me.
- I believe in myself and my abilities.
- I will remember the joy and light of my OBE.

How to Recognize and Manage Self-Doubt

The biggest barrier to your astral travel is self-doubt. Recognizing patterns and signs of doubt creeping in will help you conquer them. These can be a voice in your head telling you you can't do something, agitation, a short temper, or a reluctance to do tasks due to a lack of motivation.

When you become aware of these patterns, you'll notice the habits you've developed that lead you into this self-doubt spiral. When you hear that voice or feel debilitated and unmotivated, stop and remind yourself it's just a habit – it's not real. It's a manageable and changeable habit.

When you catch yourself going in a self-doubt loop, learn not to react. Be aware of the feeling and remove yourself mentally from the negative environment. You can do this by embracing positive physical surroundings that put you at ease. This will directly impact your psychological comfort. Find a quiet, safe, and peaceful place to give your mind time to settle down.

Try to reframe the negative emotion that continues to percolate. Challenge it by asking yourself what evidence you have to believe in these doubts. Is there proof of any of them being true? Or is it more likely that these are created in your head through fear? Now, you can release the emotion and center yourself. This thought is not real, but it can be used as part of your astral preparation learning curve. Your doubts are not a sign of inadequacy or failure. They teach you how to detach from thoughts that don't serve you and replace them with positive perspectives that aid your success.

As you mentally detach from self-doubt, you are practicing a form of separation. If you can separate from your mind's ramblings, you will soon separate from your physical senses. You could also join a community of people discovering their spiritual abilities. There, you'll share experiences and exchange tips that will alleviate your fears. A group like this provides support and a sense of normalcy about astral projection.

Reframing Fear

Your fear is trying to protect you from harm, but it's up to you to decide whether it will remain a mental block or a challenge to be unlocked. Rewiring your negative thoughts and seeing them as an opportunity for building mental resilience will help you better navigate challenges.

Notice the fear

Don't try to distract yourself from the fear. Notice where you feel it in your body. Perhaps you feel it in the pit of your stomach, making it feel physically real, but it's not. Fear is not internal but an external energy that can be removed from you. It is subjective and changeable through perspective and environment. Take this as an opportunity to determine objective reality. You created this fear, and you can make yourself feel better. It is only debilitating if you allow it to be.

Rename the Emotion

Once you evaluate the feeling, name it something constructive. Rename anxiousness into what it really is – not a hint you cannot do this, but a way your body is simply trying to prepare you. Anxiety can now be renamed: a need to prepare. Your body is telling you to prepare for "peak performance." Now, whenever you feel these emotions, consider them a sign to prepare your body for rest and your mind for freedom, work on your motivation, and take action.

Practical Exercises

Follow these practical exercises to enhance your ability to project. The more you practice visualization, the easier it'll become. You can only build confidence and learn to control your experiences through active practice.

Consider this a mental rehearsal until you're able to fully project. The more familiar you become with the process, the more comfortable it will be. You'll notice your fears are reduced as you work your way up to full projection.

Below is a series of positive and uplifting scenarios for you to visualize.

Building Your Astral Shield of Light:

1. Visualize a small sphere of light forming in the center of your chest.
2. As you breathe in, allow the light to expand outward.
3. Visualize the light growing stronger and more vibrant with each breath, eventually enveloping your entire body in a protective shield.
4. Focus on the shield's strength and the intention behind it, reinforcing the belief that you are safe and protected during your astral travel.

Facing Fearful Imagery or Entities:

1. If you encounter unsettling imagery or negative entities during an astral projection attempt, pause and focus on your breath.
2. Visualize a bright portal, a staircase, a climbing rope, or a higher-dimensional space that leads you to a peaceful, comforting environment.

3. Set a clear intention to experience only positive and constructive encounters, such as meeting guides or exploring calm landscapes.

Journal About Self-doubts/Insecurities and Release Them:
1. Write down your insecurities and fears, such as a lack of confidence or struggles with anxiety.
2. Assign an action to tackle these insecurities. Dedicate time for visualizations and the positive affirmations and practices listed above.
3. Picture your insecurities written on balloons.
4. Visualize the balloon floating away as you release your old mindset, giving you the chance to focus on your new and productive thoughts.

Overcoming your fears of astral travel should not be seen as a chore but as a fun ritual to enjoy and celebrate. With these tools, you will build a strong foundation to create new and interesting tales of the astral world. These safe and tested practices will provide you with the mindset to succeed. You'll create a comfortable atmosphere, minimizing distractions and disturbances, and become well-rested and self-assured.

This is your conscious effort to dream, to explore the beyond. You are imagining, weaving, and crafting this explorative journey. So, remind yourself that you're going to be fine. You can go anywhere you want with your thoughts. Just as your thoughts take you to places you don't want to go, controlling them puts you in the driver's seat.

Chapter 7: Working with Energy and Staying Protected

The astral plane is a realm of energy that plays a major role in your ability to converse with spiritual beings and safely return to your physical body. Learning to work with and manage energy before, during, and after your out-of-body experience prepares you for safe and effective astral exploration.

Too many people overlook the importance of energy work when trying to achieve astral projection. Practicing techniques to activate your energy body will help you develop the skills to stimulate your energy structure and awaken your higher consciousness. Your energy body is where you center, store, and exchange energy. Energy work requires a combination of a present mind, clear intentions, and awareness. Working on your energy in the physical world will make this easier in the astral realm.

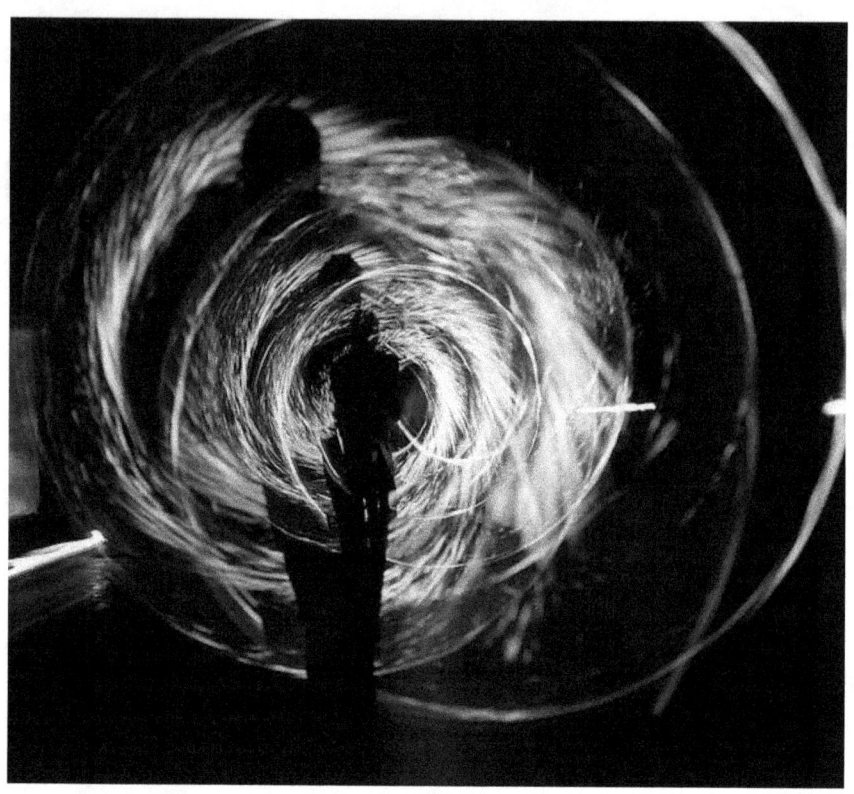

Energy awareness and flow are imperative to being in control when you're having an out-of-body experience.[17]

This chapter will teach you the foundational practices of energy awareness, energy flow, and practical measures to stay protected. When you understand energy dynamics, you will develop a secure and empowered method for navigating the astral world with intention and clarity and dismantling negative energy to safeguard your mental and emotional well-being.

The Foundational Practices of Energy

The astral body interacts with energetic currents just as the physical body does. There are three main energy fields – magnetism, electricity, and gravity. Magnetic fields fuel electric fields and vice versa, working in tandem on the same path. They are connected because one creates the other, making them almost part of the same field. Electric fields flow like a current, creating magnetic fields, and then the movement of magnets creates an electrical charge. Together, they create radiation in electromagnetic fields.

The gravitational field is potential energy preserved in an object. The object is given gravitational energy when it leaves the ground; the amount of energy only differs in regards to how close to or further away from the ground it is.

The foundations of energy in OBEs parallel these physical systems like magnetic, electric, and gravitational energy fields. Consider the magnetic field and how it determines what one attracts and repels. You can use this to your advantage, repelling unwanted energy and attracting positivity with your magnetic energy. Think of the electric field as your electric current, the energy that flows through you. As you engulf positive energy, you can feel it flowing through your body like a current, driven to every part of you through energy structures, which are like channels. Finally, gravitational energy is what will bring you closer to higher dimensions and back down to your physical body.

Energy Awareness

Energy awareness starts with being aware of everything your eyes and ears consume. Your thoughts and feelings greatly impact the energy your body retains. This, then, affects the energy you project out in the world. During your visit to the spiritual realm, this energy will impact your experience.

To become aware of energy, you must first become acquainted with the energy structure of your energy body. Your body has primary and secondary energy centers. Your primary center connects you directly to your emotions. This is why listening to music, dancing, and singing are quick ways to improve your primary energy center activity. Fun activities lead to happy energy rising through your body. The same type of energy appears when you're around people you love.

Consider how people talk about falling in love. They claim they can genuinely feel the act of falling in love. Most describe it as butterflies fluttering in their stomachs. This is energy, and it feels real because it is real.

It's not just happy sensations that trigger your energy fields. Your negative emotions are also linked to your primary energy center. This is why a broken heart can feel like a literal broken heart. People feel a physical ache. Sadness and depression can also make your heart feel physically heavy and worn out. These sensations apply during tough circumstances. This heaviness is energy stored in your chest and stomach, feeling like a burden. On the other hand, happy feelings make you feel light, as if a weight has been lifted.

Energy correlated to fear and excitement is similar. An example of your body being aware of this energy is the appearance of goosebumps all over your arms or the hair on the back of your neck standing up. You may notice your knees and legs weakening during intense fear and excitement. Fear can also loosen bowels, proving that energy is not simply in your head but has real physical consequences. The feelings and actions people associate with emotions are energy awareness.

In the same vein, what many consider a gut feeling is not merely an expression; it's intuition. Intuition is your energy body advising you on how to feel safe. It is a warning you should protect yourself from unwanted energy in your surroundings. Stress and mental pressure can fill your body with intense energy and may lead to tension headaches, back pain, and tense and cramped muscles.

You have already experienced the energy structures in your life. When you're happy, you notice the change in your energy. You feel empowered by positive emotions overflowing, and there's a pep in your step. When you're down, your energy does not empower you. Instead, that sense of heaviness and feeling drained returns, and you lack enthusiasm and hopefulness. Luckily, you can improve your energy structure through energy work.

Secondary energy centers locate the energy that flows throughout your bones and joints, from big to small. Think about how one's body interacts with energy through things like acupuncture. Undetected issues can be brought to the surface with practices like these and help people remove blockage and tension that cause them illnesses like chronic headaches and migraines. When acupuncture needles are placed in certain points of the flesh, they activate nerves and hidden energy so vital energy can flow through.

Like currents, energy flows through the channels in your body on a cellular level to your energy points, the parts of your body also known as your chakras, most commonly in your fingers, arms, legs, and forehead. These channels allow energy to surge through the core of your body. This is why those who aspire to achieve astral projection are told to use their senses to stay grounded in the astral plane. Your sense of touch, smell, sight, taste, and hearing can redirect your focus and determine where your energy is or needs to be active.

Energy Flow

Energy flow is the stimulation of energy in your body. Maintaining energy balance is significant in achieving a positive out-of-body experience, just as it is vital for achieving positive outcomes in your day-to-day activities. In both the physical and spiritual realms, you will be impacted by the energy surrounding you. Unfamiliar energy specifically can be overwhelming and overstimulate your energy flow in a way that locks negative energy inside with no way out as you struggle to settle it down. So, understanding how to ensure negative energy flows out and positive energy flows in will improve your quality of life and OBEs.

Low energy and under-stimulation can make it harder to do tasks in your daily life, and overly high energy makes it difficult to center yourself and remain calm when necessary. You must achieve equilibrium in your energy flow for optimal astral projection performance. Overactive and depleted energy states will change the outcome of your experiences.

Energy work practices, such as meditation or *Qigong* (a Chinese-based method of physical exercises and breathwork, similar to Tai Chi), will benefit you in all aspects of your life. Start working on controlling your energy and setting clear intentions daily. These practices will be your energetic beacon to help you move energy where you want it to go. In essence, your energy flow will "follow the light," so to speak. You will focus on the experience you want to have and minimize distractions.

So, how do you do that? Consider your primary and secondary energy centers as pores or portals through which energy enters and exits your body, impacting your health as much as the blood flowing through you. Now, think about where you store energy, like in the gut, heart, mind, and back. How can you make healthy energy flow in and negative energy flow out? Just as your physical body needs nutritious food to improve your health and blood flow and adapt to a healthier lifestyle, your energy body needs vital energy flow. Changing your location, being mindful of what information you consume, and removing yourself from bad situations are a few ways to improve your energy diet. Maintaining a steady energy flow is nutrition for astral projection. Just as nutrition leads to a better quality of life, a healthy energy diet leads to a strengthened astral body, helping you attune to higher vibrations.

Then, it's time to learn about energy exchange, ensuring you don't absorb energy you don't want. Many people can find themselves adapting to the energy of any room they walk into and struggle to preserve their own. Energy is exchanged through body pathways like your mouth via breathing, which is why meditative practices encourage deep breathing techniques to ease pain and discomfort and replace nervous energy with calm, collected energy to regulate your nervous system, and your feet are a portal to exchange energy because where you go alters your energy. Think of fight or flight. Your feet take you from difficult situations and enter spaces that soothe you.

Using these pathways, you will learn how to feel and move subtle energy and stay protected when astral traveling. Pathways allow energy to balance and flow, increasing frequency, raising internal vibrations, and overcoming obstacles like energy blockage and overconsumption.

Protective Measures

Protective measures are essential in creating a safe, clean, and energetic space. Without this, you won't be able to control the energy that flows in and out. Energy is consciousness. It is your emotions, imagination, intentions, and actions. This is how you relieve and receive energy. Therefore, energy does not know boundaries. You have to set them. The concept of energy boundaries requires you to lead your energetic actions. As you know, these are shaped by your thoughts and emotions and what you choose to retain in your imagination. Placing boundaries means determining the properties in your thoughts and feelings through intentional, conscious actions.

The saying goes, "Where your attention goes, your energy flows." This is energy work's fundamental principle, so the best way to protect yourself is to focus on clearing negative energy and mentally reinforcing your energy field to shield against negative influences and encounters. You don't need special skills for this. Energy runs through your body all day. All you must do is stimulate it. Your body contains powerful healing mechanisms you can tap into simply with body awareness. Through energy work exercises, you will know how to connect yourself to your higher, spiritual self and, in turn, use energy to mentally and physically heal wounds and injured areas.

Body awareness exercises will help you identify energy you do and don't want; you'll cleanse your energy body of intrusions and self-heal from previously experienced negative energy. The following measures will ensure you awaken your energy structures to stay protected during astral projection.

To clear your aura of negative vibration, take daily walks in the sunlight and dedicate ten minutes to meditating in the evenings before you sleep. This will help wire your mind and body for relaxation. Then, when you engage in meditative practices for your OBE preparation, you are already in the right state of mind.

Energy use, manipulation, and healing are how you set energetic boundaries. The goal is to safeguard your vital energy and discard what you can consider dead weight through awareness-based movement. Vital energy is what makes you feel alive and positive. It sparks your creativity and uplifts you mentally, emotionally, and spiritually. Incorporate the following principles in daily life to empower you. These will also be your go-to exercises during spiritual practices.

Practical Exercises

Sensing Your Energy Field

1. Place your hands out in front of you with your palms facing each other but not touching.
2. Slowly move your hands closer together and then farther apart. Imagine you are encouraging energy to join you as your palms move toward each other and reinforcing your control of your space as your palms move further away.
3. You might notice sensations like warmth, tingling, or a subtle pressure between your palms.
4. Focus on these sensations. They are vibrations that help you become aware of your energy field.

Practice this exercise regularly to deepen your energy sensitivity.

Setting Energetic Boundaries

1. Disengage from stressful, energetic states by walking it off or closing your eyes and focusing on breath control. This notifies your body that you will extract yourself from certain circumstances and affirms your control of your energy state.

2. Discern between emotion and empathy. Is this your concern, or are you adopting an emotion that does not align with your circumstances? If so, pride yourself on your empathy and expel the emotion as a voice or feeling that is not your own.
3. Now, speak your reality. For example, "I am at peace," "I choose which energy I invite," "I choose to repel this (emotion) and replace it with my truth," and "My mind and body do as I command."
4. Repeat your goal or intention, such as "I am going to walk towards positivity" or "I intend to seek peace with each step and breath."

Repeat this exercise when you feel a shift in your sensations, merge your feelings with others around you, or become uncertain about beliefs you know deep down is your truth.

Balancing Energy

Visualization

1. Get comfortable. Find a quiet, peaceful spot without distractions and wear loose, comfortable clothing.
2. Picture energy, making your body aware of its intention.
3. Imagine this energy bouncing around, movable, raising your awareness even higher. You can then manipulate which energy glides towards you and which you can cut off as it nears you.
4. You can sense where energy is stored, where the imbalance is, in your chest or torso, and nudge it down your arms and legs to the soles of your feet.
5. Notice the sensation as you picture yourself discarding unwanted energy and immerse yourself in the lightness of relaxation. Memorize this feeling of centeredness and balance.

Breathing

1. Close your eyes slowly. Let your eyelashes softly shut.
2. Take a deep breath that fills your lungs. If you feel tightness in your ribcage, imagine your chest opening up and dissolving agitation (nervous energy) as you slowly breathe out, getting accustomed to the ease and slowness of the flow. Repeat four to eight times.

3. Your body will start to relax, and your mind will quieten. Let this sensation envelop you.

Posturing

1. Stand in front of a mirror.
2. Straighten your spine by rolling your shoulders down and holding your neck high. Avoid tilting your pelvis forward or backward. Keep your feet hip-length apart so your pelvis and all your weight are in the center.
3. You will notice a difference in the energy you command when you're not slouched over.
4. Loosen your jaw. You can make an "ahh" sound to help you. A tightened jaw locks in tension.
5. Focus on standing tall and how it draws in calm energy and mental strength. Refer to this posture when you feel your body tense up and your energy imbalances.

Physical Movement

1. Aside from walking or dancing, stretch for five to ten minutes to release imbalanced energy.
2. Get a mat and practice a few yoga poses that stretch the muscles with the most tension. Consider the downward dog and the side-body and hip-flexor stretches.
3. These will reveal where tension is and release it.
4. Notice your body loosening up and becoming limber. Your muscles are well-rested, and your mind is liberated. This is your body restoring its energy balance.

Positive Affirmations

1. Write down intentions you want to refer to (reframing negative feelings).
2. Keep them short and succinct.
3. Get yourself in the frame of mind to believe them. Try taking a breath before you utter each affirmation.
4. Express them out loud first thing in the morning and just before bed. Older practices would consider this chanting. Chanting was known as a way to expel negative energies. Positive affirmations do the same thing in reverse. You are inviting positive energy when you speak it out into the universe.

Energy Cleansing Ritual

Prior to an OBE

1. Lay down comfortably in bed and stretch your legs. You can flex and point your toes like a ballerina to ensure your focus is on your body, not your mind.
2. You can set the room's tone with soothing music and dim lights.
3. Use crystals to repel negative energy. These can be worn or placed on your bedside table.
4. Imagine energy moving with your blood from head to toe. Be aware of your body resting as relaxing energy meets every part of it.
5. Feel a pleasant tingling sensation as energy travels down to your toes.
6. Visualize a cleansing light above you.
7. Sense its positive vibrations shining like your beacon calling you away from negative energy.
8. With a focus on your feet, imagine you're taking steps toward the light. With each step, you feel the positive reverberations of the light, creating a shield around you.

Practice this exercise regularly to redirect yourself when you feel surrounded by negativity. A similar meditative practice can be done to reach the astral plane, where the light leads you to the astral world. Then, use the following cleansing ritual during your OBE to ward off negative entities on your psychic adventures.

During an OBE

1. Bring your attention to your body to ground yourself. Become aware of your fingers by opening a fist, spread your toes so your feet carry your weight evenly, and remember the tingling sensations you felt when you practiced body awareness in bed by stretching your legs and flexing your feet.
2. Take a deep breath in and imagine this is the positive energy you felt with your crystals and soft music. As you exhale, picture bad energy leaving your body. Imagine it flowing from your head to your toes and then released, bringing you further away from the spiritual world and reconnecting with your physical body. Feel this breath exiting your body in the shape of a "J."

3. Roll your shoulders back and down and focus on your feet, imagining you can feel the earth's surface beneath you, the roots of your energy shield.
4. With this calm mindset, you can now picture your beacon of light cleansing you of unwanted energy.

Grounding Exercises

Tree Roots Technique

1. Stand with your legs hip-length apart. Feel the soles of your feet on the ground. Imagine they are tree roots anchoring your body. Picture them descending deeper into the earth, firmly planting you in the strength and safety of nature.
2. Take slow breaths, and with each one, imagine your roots growing longer, becoming embedded in the earth.
3. Focus on the relaxing feeling of these vines entwined in the earth's soil.
4. Engrave the sensation in your memory so you can return to the feeling of reconnecting with the earth whenever you wish.

White Light Technique

1. Breathe in through your nose for four counts and exhale for another four to center yourself and your energy.
2. Visualize a glowing, white light shooting out of the top of your head. It begins to travel down your body like a soft breeze.
3. It makes you feel warm and safe, reminding you that you're in control and can slow down your energy and energy that interacts with yours.
4. Feel negative thoughts or visitors during your OBE slip away into the darkness as you're surrounded by this dazzling light.
5. You then decide to absorb the white light that percolates your astral body and return to your physical one or continue your exotic journey with the light as your protective shield.

Chakras Technique

1. Bring awareness to each body part. This time, in reverse, starting with your feet and working your way up.
2. Think of each body part connecting to one of your chakras (the energy points you learned are in your body's core, enabling your energy structure).

3. Slowly inhale deeply and exhale, allowing yourself to feel sensations in each chakra until the vibrations cover your entire body, relaxing it.
4. As you relax, the surface below supports your chakras, pushing you downward as if to place you safely in bed or planting your feet in crisp grass.
5. Eventually, you reach a peaceful state as your chakras protect you from what blocks your peace.

The Third-Eye Technique

1. Imagine all your awareness rising to your third eye (the center of your forehead just above your eyebrows)
2. Focus on the area or room you're in. Picture every detail thoroughly. You can use your five senses to remove yourself from negative entities.
3. Now, visualize yourself rising above as if you're in a hot air balloon. You are free and floating in the vast blue sky. From above, you can see your body standing in the room or area, interacting with your senses and the details of the space, proving you can distance yourself and leave the astral world whenever you please.

You can use the rope technique to help picture yourself out of your body. Visualize the rope hanging from the ceiling and imagine pulling yourself up and out of your body to see what's beneath you. Since you use this method to enter or exit the astral plane, you can also use it to ground yourself if you need to refocus your energy and don't want to return to the physical world yet.

When working with energy, the goal is to allow free movement of your astral body while being able to ground your physical body. This is how you ensure you stay protected and guard from unwanted interactions and auras.

Practice energy work before your OBE exercises by setting boundaries when in negative energy states, taking breaks like a walk or stretch, setting intentions for the day, limiting distractions, and controlling what emotions you pay attention to and when. This prevents energy drainage and mind cluttering to avoid this happening during astral travel.

Chapter 8: Integrating Your OBEs

So far, you've learned how to use astral travel and intentional out-of-body experiences as tools for spiritual exploration. However, these journeys can also foster immense personal growth, especially if you integrate them into your daily spiritual practices. This chapter will show you the ins and outs of using astral projection to increase self-awareness, gain powerful insights, heal, and more. In it, you can learn how to use OBEs for whatever spiritual or personal needs you want to fulfill or goals you want to achieve.

Out-of-body experiences can greatly contribute to your personal growth.[18]

Astral Travel as a Self-Reflection Tool

Astral projection is an incredibly transformative practice because everything starts with you. Every journey prompts you to reflect on your experiences and see what you've retained from them. With regular journeying and reflecting on your thoughts, emotions, and experiences, you raise awareness of yourself. You learn who you truly are, your strengths, weaknesses, and areas of growth. As the practice requires dedication, the more effort you put into self-reflection, the easier it will be to track and notice your progress. You'll look back on your growth (whether in astral projection or spirituality in general), and you'll see where you can still do more to improve. Simultaneously, you'll learn where you have improved and what you can celebrate. Seeing how far you've come on your journey is a massive confidence booster and provides motivation for staying committed to perfecting your astral practice.

During your travels, you'll discover patterns and recurring experiences. Regular practice and self-reflection allow you to identify these patterns, analyze them, and understand their connection to your physical life. By gaining a deeper understanding of who you are, you'll also learn how you embrace the insights you've gathered, what feelings these evoke, which regular experience provokes profound emotions, etc. All this can facilitate a much smoother learning experience for mastering astral projection. Regular self-reflection through astral travel can deepen your soul's bond with its true, higher self. However, it can just as well improve your connection with your physical self. The insights you learn during your journeys are often linked to events in the physical realm.

By exploring how your astral experiences reflect on your life in the Matrix, you can get even more out of your OBEs. For example, sometimes, you'll receive guidance or answers to questions related to real-life experiences. You may learn how to achieve the goals here, even without asking how to do it there. Or, you can learn how to set intentions in a way that guides you toward the information you're looking for. If you're facing challenges or feeling stuck, you can also consult the higher planes about moving forward. Again, setting the proper intention will be crucial for getting the right answers. As always, be clear and concise when formulating your intention, and you will be able to manifest it. For example, if you're facing an obstacle you aren't sure how to overcome, start your projection attempts by stating that you wish to find a resolution for your issue.

Connection to Higher Consciousness and Gaining Insights

Through your journeys, you'll have a chance to connect to spiritual guides or your higher consciousness, either of which can be a powerful way to gain new insights. Just like spiritual guides, your higher consciousness also resides outside the Matrix. It's connected to the universal energy that envelopes everything in the higher dimensions. It can help you harness wisdom, guidance, and support for navigating the ups and downs of every journey, including life itself.

In the beginning, the insights you gain will be helpful for mastering successful astral projection. You'll receive lots of hints and messages, learn to become more aware of them, decipher them, and integrate them into your practice. By understanding how this process works, you'll be able to transfer this into your daily life, and this is where you can start using OBEs to find solutions to life's challenges.

Meditation and visualization are the most powerful ways to connect with spiritual beings or your higher self. Both practices require you to quiet your mind, relax your body, and focus on your intention. They prompt you to empower your connection with the higher dimensions with tools that enhance your experience (i.e., specific visions, breathing techniques, etc.).

Aligning with your higher self means you'll find empowerment, beauty, and enlightenment far beyond what you've experienced before. You'll be able to revel in the knowledge your true self can offer, and more importantly, you'll learn how to trust this new information you've uncovered. Living in the Matrix may keep people in ignorance, but many learn to distrust whatever they discover about their surroundings. By practicing astral projection, you'll understand how to leave this prejudice behind and simply trust that what you see and experience is the universe's truth.

Each new insight you learn expands your consciousness, which is one of the biggest benefits of astral travel. You become conscious of your choices, thoughts, emotions, and actions and how these affect and are affected by the universe. You raise your awareness of the true nature of reality, steering away from what you've been conditioned to learn in the Matrix. After all, there are infinite possibilities and countless opportunities to evolve and develop, and astral projection opens you up to exploring all of these.

The universal consciousness is everywhere, but you can only tap into it through deeply personal and elevating practices. Astral travel is one of them. It's a powerful tool for exploring the space that binds everyone and everything, but it divides everyone and everything by giving everything a unique purpose. Incidentally, astral projection allows you to understand what you are meant to achieve in life. Your experience can transform your life from the roots, making it more fulfilling and purposeful. How? Sometimes, seeing your life's path is challenging because many obstacles obscure your view. The insights you gain through astral travel can clear out the obstacles, bringing you the clarity to see what path you're meant to be walking.

Through astral travels and insights, you can establish a balance between your physical reality and the realms where you can explore new insights. This is particularly beneficial for beginners struggling with embracing the concept of dimensions beyond the Matrix because they are deeply conditioned to believe that only the physical realm exists. Even if you aren't ready to let go of some beliefs just yet, your travels can help you accept the idea that there is more to the universe. You'll know this because you'll witness it during your OBEs. Even this simple knowledge will make it easier to start integrating astral lessons into your daily life.

Creative Inspiration

In the astral realm, you can manifest your deepest desires. These manifestations can give way to creativity and inspiration in spiritual work or any other area of life. If you've already begun your artistic journey, encounters with different dimensions can unlock fresh ideas. If you haven't, they can help you uncover and grow your potential and achieve your dreams. For many, this can mean advancement in their careers but also in their personal lives. Art is a wonderful way to express feelings, needs, and desires, and mastering astral projection can help you do all of this. Getting imaginative can bring joy and fulfillment into your life even if you aren't an artist but simply love dedicating time to creative hobbies.

When you astral travel, you rely on your intuition to guide you toward universal consciousness and manifest whatever you seek. With practice, you can learn to make everything materialize almost instantly. You can then transfer this ability to your projects, as well. Do you lack ideas for a project? Manifest it like you would manifest wanting to travel to a specific location or get answers to inquiries in the astral realm.

In the higher dimensions, everything is possible. You're not limited by the constraints of the physical world. This is why you can open yourself to much more creativity and inspiration. Besides creative pursuits, you can get inspired to incorporate insights into other, broader spiritual practices, as well. Mindfulness, meditation, and other spirituality-enhancing techniques rely on intuition and manifestation. Once you learn how to make things happen in the astral, you can do it in these practices, too. For example, you can take the same steps you took to manifest something in the astral realm and apply them to your intuition to relax and gain spiritual insights through meditation. Or, you can do a quick astral projection before a mindfulness exercise and use the insights you gained on your trip for a more profound self-discovery quest.

Other Ways to Use Astral Projection

Your astral journeys will help you explore new perspectives, gain clarity over matters and situations, and learn to be more objective when approaching any circumstance. This promotes better decision-making and problem-solving abilities, allowing you to overcome any obstacle in life. Whether you are facing issues in your spiritual, personal, or professional life, astral travel can help you find a solution. For example, if you're struggling with your interpersonal relationships, insight from your astral journey may allow you to understand where the problems are coming from and how to resolve them efficiently. You can build better relationships and improve the current ones because you'll know what to do to get there.

If you wish to heal from past emotional and spiritual trauma, astral travel will allow you to find out how to do this, too. Likewise, it can help you harness the knowledge and power needed to heal others. How? Sometimes, trauma leads to deep-rooted issues that only profound reflection and exploration can uncover. To identify the root cause of your problems and release eventual traumas related to these, you need a safe space. In astral, you feel powerful, secure, and confident. You feel you can do everything, including confronting painful experiences, fears, and other powerful emotions. Moreover, you can connect with your higher self and other higher, spiritually enlightened beings who can help you find clarity on how to overcome your trauma and heal. They can empower you to overcome everything and move forward with a healthier and happier life. Do you know what else happens during astral travel? Before you even start the separation, you focus on your vibrations. You concentrate on raising them (especially if you want to communicate with higher beings) and enriching them with positivity so you can attract more positivity during your journey. By elevating your vibrational energy, you've already begun the healing process. Through the insights you gain during travels, you can learn how to form intentions to harness healing energy and use it to revitalize specific energetic imbalances or heal spiritual wounds. You'll heal on a deep level because your healing starts with your energy and your spiritual body, which is the first one that gets empowered in astral travel.

Daily OBE Integration Ritual

This ritual will help you integrate your out-of-body experiences into your daily schedule, giving you a head start on your journey of mastering purposeful and regular astral projection. Essentially, it's a combination of journaling, setting intentions, and a brief mindfulness practice.

Instructions:
1. Start your mornings by writing about how your astral insights relate to your current goals or challenges. Do this for 5-10 minutes right after waking up. This is when your mind is not yet clouded with the worries of the day, and you can easily tap into your intuition.
2. Then, move on to setting an intention for the day. Center your intention on the insight you've uncovered during the previous minutes of reflection. For example, if you want to learn more about how to focus your astral journeys toward resolving an issue, make this your intention for future travels.
3. Repeat the intention in your mind or out loud three times.
4. Take a deep breath and let it out slowly. Take another deep breath, focusing on feeling the ground beneath your feet.

5. With each breath you take, you feel yourself becoming more and more centered, ready to take on the day's challenges, including gaining new astral insights.

Healing with OBEs

With the right approach, astral travel can lead to incredibly transformative and healing experiences. The following exercise will teach you how to set out on a journey with the intention to heal and garner as much love and compassion as possible – for yourself and everyone else.

Instructions:
1. Find a quiet and comfortable space. Then, close your eyes and deepen your breathing.
2. Relax your body and mind and focus on your breathing.
3. Think about a past emotional wound or trauma you wish to heal from. Visualize how and when it occurred, how it affected you, or whatever image you want to associate with the trauma.
4. Then, as you relax more and more, imagine that you can journey to a place where you can safely explore and face your trauma. Set the intention for needing a safe space and repeat it.
5. Connect with the positive energies around you, and let them guide you through the separation process.
6. Once you're in the astral plane, think about your trauma again. What emotions and thoughts does it evoke in you? Bringing them up may be painful, but it's necessary. You can only let go of something you know you're holding onto.
7. Visualize a beam of light enveloping you, a little dim at first but still glowing with a golden sheen.
8. Now, imagine that all those emotions and feelings slowly leave your body. With each painful one you release, the light around you becomes a little brighter.
9. Repeat until the light shines bright like golden sunshine, and you no longer feel the burden of your trauma. You may not be able to do this in one journey, and that's okay. You can always repeat it until you can let go of everything.
10. Once you feel you've let go of everything you could, return to your physical body.

11. Continue to take deep breaths to ground yourself. Feel yourself becoming anchored to the earth, rejuvenated, and stronger than ever.

Creative Inspiration Exercise

Practicing astral projection requires a lot of intuitive work. By honing your intuition, you're also boosting your creativity. If you struggle with finding inspiration for your creative pursuits, you may discover it with the help of astral travel. The following exercise will help you get those creative juices flowing.

Instructions:
1. Sit comfortably and focus on a specific creative project.
2. Draw a few deep breaths, and let your eyes close on their own as your body and mind relax.
3. Visualize yourself leaving your body and stepping into the astral plane. Imagine you can go to a place where you can encounter creative inspiration – focus on this, and you'll soon find yourself in a new environment.
4. Look around. See if you can notice any symbols or ideas that may inspire you. Tap into the energies around you. How do they feel? Do they feel enlightening in some way? What does your gut tell you about them? You may have a sudden new idea on how to proceed with the project. Or, you may encounter symbols that can give you a clue on how to proceed.
5. Spend as much time roaming around as you need to find the inspiration you're looking for.
6. When you're ready to come back, set the intention for returning to your body, and you'll be back in no time.
7. Once you're back, grab a piece of paper and jot down everything you saw and any ideas that came to you. Try to recall as many vivid details as possible.

Decision-Making Through Astral Clarity

Making informed decisions isn't always easy in the Matrix. By journeying with the intention of gaining clarity and connecting with others in the higher planes, you can gain knowledge to decide on the best course of action in every situation. The other entities can offer wisdom from the vast consciousness around everyone and everything. Your journeys can be as enlightening as you want them to be, and they can give you the answers you're looking for just when you need them. The higher realms are vast and mysterious, full of knowledge. Learn how to harness this knowledge through the following meditation.

Instructions:
1. Assume a comfortable position and relax by taking several deep breaths. Close your eyes.
2. Think about a decision you struggle to make or a dilemma in front of you. Bring whatever you're indecisive or unsure about to the forefront of your mind. Focus on it.
3. Formulate your intention based on what you need the resolution for. For example, if you can't make a decision, you can say, "I need help making a decision about..."
4. Focus on your intention and relax your mind and body even more. Keep breathing deeply until you reach a profound state of relaxation where you can only feel the humming vibrations of your body and the energy around you.
5. When you feel the vibrations, tap into them. Repeat your intention, and let it guide you to a place where you can manifest it (the space in the astral realm where you can get the resolution you seek).
6. Suddenly, you feel you've arrived at a place where everything feels different. The vibrations are different. You feel differently, and you know you've left the physical realm.
7. Send your intention out to the space around you. Your spiritual guides will come to you and offer their assistance. Or, you can call on them or your higher self.
8. As you wait for the arrival of the helpful entities, consider your dilemma or decision. Try to approach it from different angles. This will help the entities, too - they'll be better equipped to help once they know your struggles and views about the subject.
9. Once your spiritual guide arrives or you connect to your higher self, state what you need to get resolved. Wait for the answers. You may receive messages right away, giving you a clue on how to make the decision ahead of you. Be open to any form of communication or wisdom you may receive. By being receptive to any information you can gain from the astral realms, you can

gain more profound insights into any question or issue.

10. Once you feel you received all the answers or assistance you could, thank whoever assisted you (even your higher self) and set the intention of returning to your physical body.

11. Reflect on the insights you gained during your journey. You may be unable to decipher all the messages you've received. That is okay. You can always record them in a journal. Then, once you record insights you've gained through several journeys, you can revisit them and see if you can gain a new perspective and make the decision you struggled with.

Enhancing Spiritual Life through OBEs

Visualization is an incredibly useful tool in spiritual practices, especially if you want to connect and harness wisdom from higher realms (whether from guides or the universal consciousness).

Instructions:

1. In a distraction-free environment, find a comfy position and take deep breaths until your body and mind relax.

2. Let your eyes drift close naturally, and continue breathing deeply. As you do, set the intention to visit a higher realm.

3. When you've reached a profound state of relaxation, visualize yourself traveling to this realm.

4. As you arrive, you notice you are enveloped in a warm, golden light. It makes you feel loved, safe, and empowered. You instantly know it can give you anything you ask for - any insight, guidance, or answer you seek. This light is the universal energy.

5. You feel the energy permeating every fiber of your being, filling you with positivity and wisdom.

6. Focus on feeling this energy in and around you. You may feel it buzz through you. Or, you may have another sensation coursing through you. Whatever it is, concentrate on it.

7. Now, tap into the energy and state the intention of wanting to connect to a spiritual being/higher consciousness. Repeat until you notice the signs of being connected to another energy source. This may be the feeling of being more empowered, abundant positivity flowing toward you, or the sensation of having something or someone close to you.

8. When you feel/sense/or see your connection materializing with this entity, ask them how to deepen your spiritual practice. Ask them how to raise your self-awareness and find inner peace. You can also ask for advice for specific spiritual practices like meditation.
9. Focus on maintaining the connection until you feel you've received answers to all your questions. Then, let go of the connection and set the intention of slowly returning to your physical body.

Daily Matrix Escape

While you're free to practice astral projection as frequently as your energy allows, you'll likely take some days off. However, this doesn't mean you can't escape the Matrix these days. With this simple technique, you can leave the physical realm for a few moments whenever you feel overwhelmed or stressed. These brief occasions will be enough to free yourself and recharge so you can face the challenges that caused you to leave.

Instructions:
1. Find a quiet space where you can relax for a few minutes.
2. Take a few deep breaths until you feel the tension leave your body, and your mind becomes calm and relaxed.
3. Then, visualize a door or portal in your mind's eye. This portal leads to another realm. Tell yourself you want to cross the portal to reinforce your intention.
4. See yourself walking through this portal, leaving behind the constraints of your physical world.
5. Once you've crossed the portal, explore the new environment. What do you see? What do you hear? What sensations can you experience? Is there anything unusual you can pick up with your senses?
6. When you're done exploring, see yourself walking back on the same path that led you there. Let the portal take you back to your starting point.
7. After you arrive at the starting point, look at the door to memorize it. Focus on it and tell yourself you can go through that door anytime you wish.

8. Next time you feel overwhelmed again, visualize that door. It will take you to the realm you've explored right away.
9. Record your experience in a journal. Write about the feelings and thoughts you had when you went to the astral plane. How did it feel to leave the Matrix? What did you learn during your journey? Record any insights you've discovered. It will help you track your progress and growth.

Conclusion

If you don't know what to expect, an out-of-body experience can be daunting and frightening. Fearing the unknown is natural. However, now that you understand the purpose of astral projection and how it works, you can safely explore higher dimensions and see why seeking astral travel is worth it.

The world is not meant to be perfectly understood but explored and challenged. With OBEs, you can find answers to all your questions, understand your life and the world better, and tailor your experiences in a way that suits you best.

Now that you have come to the end of this in-depth guide, you know how to lead your life with intention. You have acquired the knowledge that can make your fantasies and dreams a reality. These are priceless lessons that only your astral self can learn, and they will shape your physical world for the better.

This book took you on an adventure to explore the significance of your unconscious. It taught you about the Matrix and how astral projection can help you uncover truths. With actionable techniques, you saw how to escape the prism of the Matrix and identify the nature vs nurture aspects of everything you knew. Then, you were led to seek the ultimate knowledge, discovering the importance of spiritual dimensions, where you receive all the substantial ways you can enrich your life, gain more prominent perspectives on your views regarding reality, death, and the afterlife, and improve your emotional, mental, and physical health.

You learned the quantum science of an out-of-body experience. Any disbelief or misconceptions you had about connection and spirituality were resolved, and the historical and philosophical aspects of journeying beyond the Matrix were explained, making even the most skeptical of people believe that this isn't nonsense.

This book prepared you to venture beyond your physical body. This is your roadmap to understanding and channeling your emotions. You learned to face your vulnerabilities through the exercises provided, how to turn your fear into preparation, how you can morph caution into curiosity and excitement, and how your doubts can be diminished and replaced with determination. Through practice, visualization, prayer, and concentration, you learned how to strengthen your beliefs and self-esteem.

The following chapter walked you through your first OBE on the astral plane so you know what to expect. It dispelled your fears of starting something new through safe practices. You now know what astral projection feels like. You can picture your astral body as a ghostly figure floating and flying up to spiritual realms. You can pass through solid objects, including walls, and observe your physical body in the same way you would an inanimate object.

This book helped set you on the path to freedom and self-acceptance, offering healthy ways to take your power back. You received guidance on exploring dimensions beyond the earthly Matrix, recognized your potential–and the universe's potential–and how to navigate through darkness into light.

You then discovered how to overcome fear and barriers to astral travel. While some people have had bad experiences due to unintentional OBEs, such as near-death experiences, you can rest assured that intentional astral travel is entirely different.

You have the tools to not react to your anxieties, to address challenges, and to heal inner wounds. You also learned to manage and reframe your fears, doubts, and triggers. You can now face any obstacles or negative images in your way with protective practices and positive affirmations.

As you learned in this guide, you have an avenue for profound insight in the form of an intentional out-of-body experience. This insight has lasting effects, resulting in you living a fulfilling life.

The exercises in this book showed you how to work with energy and stay protected. You are well-prepared to safely face the unknown. You know of the methods to transform the energy around you and your own, finding that there is no limit to your mind and imagination. As a result, you know how to develop a positive outlook and define your life with your own style, philosophies, and authenticity.

Lastly, you were taught how to integrate your out-of-body experiences. The lessons in the last chapter can empower your personal and spiritual growth. Your personal life will benefit from your newfound capabilities and courage.

You have learned there are many practical benefits to OBEs and how they have transformed people's lives and impacted everything from studies to jobs. Astral projection has been known to solve crimes, combat terrorism, explore the psychology of criminals, and aid scientific research. The psychic abilities gained through astral travel have even helped people find missing pets and children. You can now explore your psychic talents and apply what you have learned to help those around you.

This detailed guide proved that astral projection can give your life meaning. You will come away from this valuing life lessons, experiences, and relationships, rather than material possessions. This book also taught you how to communicate with deceased loved ones and spiritual beings you can look to for guidance.

These tried and tested methods will seem designed for you once you see how successful they are. This book contains everything you need to be the creative, passionate explorer you were meant to be.

Like all extraordinary journeys, this requires time and effort. You cannot simply read this book and expect your body to magically know what to do. It is a process that requires patience and practice. Experience and time trump thoughts. So, instead of simply thinking about it, put in the work to meditate, visualize, and believe. Then, each experience will bring you closer to your goals. The skills you attain will give you confidence, and you'll soon be exploring the beauty, thrill, and mystery of the universe.

Your life is full of highs, lows, moments of defeat, triumphs, successes, and losses. Astral projection helps you make sense of it all and find strength where you least expect it. It will teach you to craft the life you want and create meaningful, precious moments.

You are well on your way to becoming a seasoned astral projector who can explore their unconscious and exotic realms as they please. Each time you embark on these travels, you will gain an even bigger understanding of the astral plane. Your out-of-body experiences become effortless. You will breathe a soft sigh of relief because you know how easy it is to dissolve your fears.

So, continue to harvest all you've worked for, reflect on the teachings in this book, and realize you can overcome any obstacles in your way. You are surrounded by an abundance of joy and beauty and can determine the energy around you. Feed your positive energy, embrace change, and remember that every surprise that unfolds along the way is full of opportunities. Let go of your fear of uncertainty and choose growth. Out-of-body experiences prove that the greatest things in life arrive to us unannounced.

If you enjoyed this book, I'd greatly appreciate a review on Amazon because it helps me to create more books that people want. It would mean a lot to hear from you.

To leave a review:
1. Open your camera app.
2. Point your mobile device at the QR code.
3. The review page will appear in your web browser.

Thanks for your support!

Here's another book by Mari Silva that you might like

Your Free Gift
(only available for a limited time)

Thanks for getting this book! If you want to learn more about various spirituality topics, then join Mari Silva's community and get a free guided meditation MP3 for awakening your third eye. This guided meditation mp3 is designed to open and strengthen ones third eye so you can experience a higher state of consciousness. Simply visit the link below the image to get started.

https://spiritualityspot.com/meditation

Or, Scan the QR code!

References

10 Tips to Astral Project Safely. IAC International Academy of Consciousness. https://www.iacworld.org/10-tips-for-astral-projection/

20-Minute Astral Travel Meditation to Connect With Your Future Self. (2024, November 4). Insight Timer Blog. https://insighttimer.com/blog/connect-to-your-future-self-astral-travel-meditation/

Alkhafaji, B. (2017, March 26). Out-of-body-experiences: a phenomenological comparison of different causes. Academia.edu. https://www.academia.edu/32048293/Out_of_body_experiences_a_phenomenological_comparison_of_different_causes

Allison. (2019, December 31). The Sleeping Third. The Sleeping Third. https://thesleepingthird.com/blog/floatingthroughthecosmos

Amanda. (2019, September 2). Connect to the Astral Network of Abundance. Chakra Center. https://chakracenter.org/2019/09/02/connect-to-the-astral-network-of-abundance/

Astral Projection Diet: It's NOT as Difficult as You Think | elephant journal. (2020, November 25). Elephant Journal | Daily Blog, Videos, E-Newsletter & Magazine on Yoga + Organics + Green Living + Non-New Agey Spirituality + Ecofashion + Conscious Consumerism=It's about the Mindful Life. https://www.elephantjournal.com/2020/11/astral-projection-diet-its-not-as-difficult-as-you-think/

Astral Projection: The Ultimate Guide for Beginners. (2023). Tiny Rituals. https://tinyrituals.co/blogs/tiny-rituals/astral-projection?srsltid=AfmBOood5g2czuh55DOodCXBnuA0Wm285cGuIQAQDxKobT-vRv9NtdIf

Baker, E. M. (2024, November 11). A Witches Guide to Successful Astral Projection - City Witch. City Witch. https://www.citywitch.co.uk/successful-astral-projection

Bellec, Y. (2024, July 14). The Pineal Gland, a Global Review of Its Functions and Its Relationship With Spiritual Practices. Ssrn.com. https://papers.ssrn.com/sol3/papers.cfm?abstract_id=4895205

Black, F. (2022, June 4). A Guided Meditation — - White Light Exercise - Freya Black - Medium. Medium. https://medium.com/@scvaswani/a-guided-meditation-white-light-exercise-1a2acf8287f1

Blackmore S.J. (1982, January 1). Beyond the body. An investigation of out-of-body experiences. London: Heinemann. https://www.researchgate.net/publication/267209455_Beyond_the_body_An_investigation_of_out-of-body_experiences_London_Heinemann

Blackmore, S. (2020, May 29). Psychedelics and the Out-of-Body Experience | Psychology Today. Www.psychologytoday.com. https://www.psychologytoday.com/us/blog/ten-zen-questions/202005/psychedelics-and-the-out-body-experience

Blackmore, S., & Troscianko, E. T. (2018). Consciousness An Introduction. Milton Routledge.

Blanke, O. (2004). Out of body experiences and their neural basis. BMJ, 329(7480), 1414–1415. https://doi.org/10.1136/bmj.329.7480.1414

Blanke, O., Ortigue, S., Landis, T., & Seeck, M. (2002). Stimulating illusory own-body perceptions. Nature, 419(6904), 269–270. https://doi.org/10.1038/419269a

Buckley, L. (2021, April 30). Astral Projection: Is It Real? The Sleep Matters Club. https://www.dreams.co.uk/sleep-matters-club/astral-projection

Bünning, S., & Blanke, O. (2005, January 1). The out-of-body experience: precipitating factors and neural correlates (S. Laureys, Ed.). ScienceDirect; Elsevier. https://www.sciencedirect.com/science/article/abs/pii/S0079612305500244

Campillo-Ferrer, T., Alcaraz-Sánchez, A., Demšar, E., Wu, H.-P., Dresler, M., Windt, J., & Blanke, O. (2024). Out-of-body experiences in relation to lucid dreaming and sleep paralysis: A theoretical review and conceptual model. Neuroscience & Biobehavioral Reviews, 163, 105770–105770. https://doi.org/10.1016/j.neubiorev.2024.105770

Carhart-Harris, R. L. (2018). How do psychedelics work? Current Opinion in Psychiatry, 32(1), 1. https://doi.org/10.1097/yco.0000000000000467

Centre of Excellence. (2024, March 22). Astral Projection: How to Have an Out of Body Experience - Centre of Excellence. Www.centreofexcellence.com. https://www.centreofexcellence.com/astral-projection-out-of-body-experience/

Cybereality. (2022, March 14). The Matrix is real, but it's not what you think...» cybereality. Cybereality. https://cybereality.com/the-Matrix-is-real-but-its-not-what-you-think/

Dedes, J. (2019, December 2). Soul Flight - Jamie Dedes - Medium. Medium. https://medium.com/@JamieDedes/soul-flight-e6c256ec294b

Elite Learning. (2021, May 12). The Body's Energy Centers - Elite Learning. Elite Learning. https://www.elitelearning.com/resource-center/rehabilitation-therapy/the-bodys-energy-centers/

First, M. (2021, January 29). Hannah Miller Artist. Hannah Miller Artist. https://www.hannahmillerartist.com/blogformyinnerandouterjourneys/astralprojection/outofbodyexperience1?srsltid=AfmBOoohT7BvnK44tKXRo9BMq07QWXjy0hs3RYyt3n19GTofuWR3AJQN

Fraser, M. (2023, April 4). From the Physical to the Spiritual: Navigating the Planes of Existence - Matt Fraser. Meet Matt Fraser. https://meetmattfraser.com/from-the-physical-to-the-spiritual-navigating-the-planes-of-existence/

Fraser, M. (2024, October 5). Soul Journeys: Understanding Astral Projection - Matt Fraser. Meet Matt Fraser. https://meetmattfraser.com/167550-2/

Greyson, B. (2006). NEAR-DEATH EXPERIENCES AND SPIRITUALITY. Zygon, 41(2), 393–414. https://doi.org/10.1111/j.1467-9744.2005.00745.x

Grof, S. (2016, October 22). The Evidence For Non-Local Consciousness: Beyond the Brain. Conscious Lifestyle Magazine. https://www.consciouslifestylemag.com/non-local-consciousness-and-the-brain/

Harshvardhan. (2020, January 9). How Can I Develop My Astral Sense Perceptions? Ananda. https://www.ananda.org/ask/how-can-i-develop-my-astral-sense-perceptions/

How to astral project for beginners in 3 easy steps – Reaprendentia. (2020). Reaprendentia.org. https://www.reaprendentia.org/how-to-astral-project-for-beginners-in-3-easy-steps/

Howard, A. (2022, April 19). Meditation Can Change Your Brain Waves: Here's How. Psych Central. https://psychcentral.com/health/meditation-brain-waves#what-happens-in-the-brain

Insight Network, Inc. (2025). Insight Timer - #1 Free Meditation App for Sleep, Relax & More. Insighttimer.com. https://insighttimer.com/libertibreathwork/guided-meditations/third-eye-pineal-gland-activation

Insight Network, Inc. (2025a). Insight Timer - #1 Free Meditation App for Sleep, Relax & More. Insighttimer.com.

https://insighttimer.com/fredrikstangeland/guided-meditations/guided-astral-projection-floating-balloon-technique

Insight Network, Inc. (2025a). Insight Timer - #1 Free Meditation App for Sleep, Relax & More. Insighttimer.com. https://insighttimer.com/daphnegarrido/guided-meditations/journey-into-space-connect-with-higher-dimensional-beings-2

Insight Network, Inc. (2025b). Insight Timer - #1 Free Meditation App for Sleep, Relax & More. Insighttimer.com. https://insighttimer.com/fredrikstangeland/guided-meditations/astral-travel-meditation-robert-monroe-technique

Insight Network, Inc. (2025b). Insight Timer - #1 Free Meditation App for Sleep, Relax & More. Insighttimer.com. https://insighttimer.com/wilde108/guided-meditations/astral-travel-to-the-planets-for-gifts

invinciblelight. (2022). Astral Projection - The Way To Astral Realm — - Steemit. Steemit.com; Steemit. https://steemit.com/astral-projection/@invinciblelight/astral-projection-the-way-to-astral-realm-20177311151730639z

Jin Chuan, B. (2020, August 3). Are We Living in the Matrix? - A Buddhist Response. Dharma Realm Buddhist University. https://www.drbu.edu/news/are-we-living-in-the-Matrix-a-buddhist-response/

Kibibi, A. (n.d.). Squeaky Clean: Five Ways to Cleanse Your Energy. NYWICI. https://nywici.org/advance/career/squeaky-clean-five-ways-to-cleanse-your-energy/

Larkin, B. (2023). Astral Projection: The Ultimate Guide for Beginners. Tiny Rituals. https://tinyrituals.co/blogs/tiny-rituals/astral-projection?srsltid=AfmBOoonPnfFGZ8xxstn6cDueKUcewsPrDpfyvSQlLefDJhVhH4Ea028

Leadbeater, C. W. (2019). The Astral Plane. Good Press.

Llewellyn. (2008, July 22). Finding Your Akashic Records. Llewellyn Worldwide, Ltd. https://www.llewellyn.com/journal/article/1703?srsltid=AfmBOopB_KcYSQ46VMSVh2fz0EOlAedYIBsRBjzVAkWUAdkq6tSHDQDg

Marossero, D. (2023, September 6). Journeying beyond: My first "voluntary" travel to other realms through Astral Projection. Medium. https://dorotheemarossero.medium.com/journeying-beyond-my-first-voluntary-travel-to-other-realms-through-astral-projection-d41a07f40086

Moritz, J. (2022, April 19). Can Thoughts Exist Outside the Brain? John Templeton Foundation. https://www.templeton.org/news/can-thoughts-exist-outside-the-brain

Muldoon, S. (2013). The Phenomena of Astral Projection. Read Books Ltd. https://archive.org/details/muldoon-the-phenomena-of-astral-projection-optimized

Najim Mostamand. (2024, October 21). Traveling to Higher Dimensions: A Journey of Spiritual Awakening. Medium. https://namostamand.medium.com/traveling-to-higher-dimensions-a-journey-of-spiritual-awakening-e5809be80c1b

Nicholas A French. Nicholas Aa French. https://nicholasafrench.com/blog/overcoming-fear-in-astral-projection-a-guide-to-confident-exploration

Overcoming Obstacles to Astral Projection. (2022). Chicago Gnosis. https://chicagognosis.org/lectures/overcoming-obstacles-to-astral-projection

Pavlina, E. (2006, February 8). Astral Projection: My First Experience • Erin Pavlina, Intuitive Counselor. Erin Pavlina, Intuitive Counselor. https://www.erinpavlina.com/blog/2006/02/astral-projection-my-first-experience/

Pavlina, E. (2006, February 8). Astral Projection: My First Experience • Erin Pavlina, Intuitive Counselor. Erin Pavlina, Intuitive Counselor. https://www.erinpavlina.com/blog/2006/02/astral-projection-my-first-experience/

Prana Sutra. (2022, July 20). Three Bodies in Yoga: Sthula, Sukshma, and Karana Sharira. Prana Sutra Yoga. https://www.prana-sutra.com/post/sthula-sukshma-karana-sharira

Raduga, M., Kuyava, O., & Sevcenko, N. (2020). Is there a relation among REM sleep sleep-dissociated phenomena, like lucid dreaming, sleep paralysis, out-of-body experiences, and false awakening? Medical Hypotheses, 144, 110169. https://doi.org/10.1016/j.mehy.2020.110169

Robbins, L. (2018, January 28). Energetic Boundaries: 5 Boundary Setting Tricks - Wild Tree Wellness. Wild Tree Wellness. https://wildtreewellness.com/energetic-boundaries/

StJohn, G. (2017). DMT Gland. International Journal for the Study of New Religions, 7(2), 153-174. https://doi.org/10.1558/ijsnr.v7i2.31949

WiredForALegendaryLife. (2023, September 11). Exploring Astral Projection for Spiritual Enlightenment. Medium. https://medium.com/@mail_2138/exploring-astral-projection-for-spiritual-enlightenment-874d0fce20f2

Zekavati, V. (2025, February 20). Mastering Astral Projection - NLP Radio. Nlpradio.org. https://www.nlpradio.org/self-knowledge/mastering-astral-projection/

Zekavati, V. (2025, February 20). Mastering Astral Projection - NLP Radio. Nlpradio.org. https://www.nlpradio.org/self-knowledge/mastering-astral-projection/

Zekavati, V. (2025, February 20). Mastering Astral Projection – NLP Radio. Nlpradio.org. https://www.nlpradio.org/self-knowledge/mastering-astral-projection/

Zhi, G., & Rulin Xiu. (2023). Quantum Theory of Consciousness. Journal of Applied Mathematics and Physics, 11(09), 2652–2670. https://doi.org/10.4236/jamp.2023.119174

Zuk, J. (2024, May 28). What Are Light Beings? Plus, How to Communicate With Them. WikiHow. https://www.wikihow.com/Light-Beings

Image Sources

1. Photo by Ron Lach : https://www.pexels.com/photo/back-view-of-a-teen-boy-with-a-digital-background-9783353/
2. Photo by Mikhail Nilov: https://www.pexels.com/photo/woman-in-red-dress-holding-fire-6931866/
3. Photo by Pixabay: https://www.pexels.com/photo/clear-glass-with-red-sand-grainer-39396/
4. Designed by Freepik. https://www.freepik.com/free-photo/human-brain-medical-digital-illustration_15559497.htm#fromView=search&page=1&position=18&uuid=f50786fd-6b3a-4996-9195-5cc37c9aa699&query=brain
5. Photo by Amy Treasure on Unsplash https://unsplash.com/photos/woman-in-yellow-and-teal-top-sleeping-beside-lavenders-4aSCchQ1hzk
6. Designed by Freepik. https://www.freepik.com/free-photo/hearing-issues-collage-design_33536006.htm#fromView=search&page=2&position=16&uuid=a8886d8c-9b2e-4fbe-ad28-624a0c67cdaa&query=brain+waves
7. odisea2008, Attribution-NonCommercial-NoDerivs 2.0 Generic, CC BY-NC-ND 2.0, <https://creativecommons.org/licenses/by-nc-nd/2.0/deed.en> https://www.flickr.com/photos/odisea2008/8475129777
8. Photo by Alina Vilchenko: https://www.pexels.com/photo/white-and-gray-stone-on-brown-wooden-table-3610752/
9. Photo by Alex P: https://www.pexels.com/photo/woman-closing-her-eyes-against-sun-light-standing-near-purple-petaled-flower-plant-321576/
10. Photo by Polina : https://www.pexels.com/photo/an-open-notebook-with-pen-5546879/

11. Designed by azerbaijan_stockers on Freepik. https://www.freepik.com/free-photo/fashion-model-white-dress-flying-illustration_8346919.htm#fromView=search&page=1&position=12&uuid=cbc4034f-99dd-4da2-91f5-0bbe8728ffcd&query=out+of+body
12. Photo by Alex Hussein: https://www.pexels.com/photo/man-about-to-climb-using-brown-rope-2685043/
13. Photo by Alex Hussein: https://www.pexels.com/photo/man-about-to-climb-using-brown-rope-2685043/
14. Photo by Bob Price : https://www.pexels.com/photo/man-walking-on-floor-764880/
15. Photo by Toni Ivanov: https://www.pexels.com/photo/worm-s-eye-view-of-building-under-a-starry-night-1454379/
16. Photo by Evelyn Chong : https://www.pexels.com/photo/man-holding-brown-rope-1458696/
17. Photo by Pixabay: https://www.pexels.com/photo/silhouette-of-person-holding-sparkler-digital-wallpaepr-266429/
18. Photo by Tiến Nguyễn: https://www.pexels.com/photo/artistic-portrait-with-flowers-and-dreamy-effect-31716533/

www.ingramcontent.com/pod-product-compliance
Lightning Source LLC
Chambersburg PA
CBHW051846160426
43209CB00006B/1185